Advance Praise

"I'm back from a glorious five days in the woods of upstate Washington. A month ago, I didn't even know this place existed, but when I read about it in this book, something in me knew I needed to be there too. There have been few adventures that have touched me the way this one did. I'm bringing back home with me the embodiment of magic, inspiration, adventure, and even more love. "

> **—Toni Carbone**
> Life Coach and Soulo Adventurer,
> *From the Soul Coaching*

"I enjoyed GO: Solo Travel for Women *so much, I read it in one day. I relate to the author's stories about camping, overcoming her fear of heights, yoga, and traveling with her dog. This book is light-hearted and meant to inspire, and it certainly gave me a fresh perspective on approaching travel. The author gives you steps to follow and reflective questions to consider so you can find your way."

> **—Melina Marie**
> Owner, Save Earth Products

"OMGosh. I couldn't stop reading 'til the last letter on the last page. I felt like I was there, clinging to the rock wall, walking in the sand, taking the tent down in the rain. The story itself is amazing, but I loved how the author tied her Wisely Wild tips into everyday life. Those became tips I can use to get me going. Life excites me again, and I can't wait for more. This book has restored my courage to release myself to live my heart's desire!"

> **—Linda Clark**

GO

Be Nice.
Be Wild!

Danya Douse

GO

Sacred Solo Travel for Women

BY SONYA LOUISE

UN-SETTLING BOOKS
Boulder, Colorado USA

DISCLAIMER:
No part of this publication may be reproduced or transmitted in any form or by any means, mechanical or electronic, including photocopying or recording, or by any information storage and retrieval system, or transmitted in email without permission in writing from the author.

Neither the author nor the publisher assumes any responsibility for errors, omissions, or contrary interpretations of the subject matter herein. Any perceived slight of any individual or organization is purely unintentional.

Brand and product names are trademarks or registered trademarks of their respective owners.

Cover Design: Jennifer Stimson; Sally Wright Day
Typography: Sally Wright Day
Editing: Maggie McReynolds
Author's photo courtesy of James Loving Photography

For my mom, Linda Louise,
whose name means Beautiful Warrior.

She is the reason I became brave.
I am her namesake.

Contents

Introduction

*"There is something terribly mysterious, terribly
dangerous and terribly frightening about the
aspect of the wild.... We are all infected with a
yearning for a wild freedom.... Wild meaning
natural. Wild meaning being connected to one's
instincts, being connected to one's deepest soul....
There is in all women a wild and ancient gypsy
that cries in anguish when we starch her flat....
There is a part of us that can never, ever be happy
until the gypsy can dance."*

—CLARISSA PINKOLA ESTES,
WOMEN WHO RUN WITH THE WOLVES

Do you feel the rumblings? Somewhere deep inside
is an inexplicable urge to venture out alone into
the wilderness, to dive deep with Self. Maybe that
urge feels like a need for adventure, to be bold and brave and
strong. Maybe that urge feels like a need for freedom, a yearning for wide-open spaces and skies that soar. Maybe it simply
feels like a need for peace, a long, quiet pause in which the
noise and the chaos of life drifts away.

But you could never actually GO on the kind of sacred

solo journey you read about. You relish the idea in your mind, feed on the stories you hear, but you couldn't fathom the reality. You have serious obligations. You have a mortgage and a car payment. You have too many people who depend on you. You are a responsible, respectable woman who has built a life you can be proud of. And you should be proud of yourself.

You are a force to be reckoned with. You can talk-to-text sixty words per minute, deliver the flawless annual report, and clear the paper jam in the printer. While advancing your career, you take a weekend workshop on website copywriting and cheer for your niece in her first field hockey game. You organize the community shoe drive for needy families, belong to a book (wine) club, use energy-saving light bulbs, and buy Girl Scout cookies from the cuties at the supermarket. It boggles the mind what you can accomplish, all the while wearing your pencil skirt and peep-toe pumps. The problem is, you are a little too good at what you do.

You have a hard time saying no. And deep down, you don't feel like a force at all. You feel *forced*. You force your way out of bed in the morning. You force your car out of the driveway. You force yourself to focus. You force yourself to smile. You force yourself to believe that you can keep this up. You try harder, move faster, stay longer, but it never seems to be enough.

The reality is, your life is a speeding locomotive, and you are certain that if you step away from the engine, the carnage would be the stuff of headlines. So you do what is necessary, day in and day out: getting up early, staying up late, and spinning your gears in your sleep. As deep as that inner yearning is to get away, your need to maintain the life you've worked so hard for overpowers it. So instead you launder your clothes and reply to emails and ignore those inner rumblings. But they don't go away, do they?

Maybe you treat yourself to a mani/pedi every now and then, losing yourself in the spa serenity music, the hot jets of water on your feet, the kneading, vibrating massage up and down your spine. Maybe you've taken up meditation or a yoga practice. You've bought the mat and the leggings, and applaud yourself when you can squeeze in a session once a week. You get a little hung up on keeping your balance and getting your poses just right, but it feels good to breathe. It feels soooo good to just breathe. For a moment, just for this moment, no one needs anything from you. The moment is fleeting.

I suspect that every now and then it gets to be just a little too much. The weight of your world bears down on you, and that deep, inner urge fires in your gut. Your thoughts start racing, and your breathing goes shallow. Your chest feels tight. Your hands feel quick and itchy, your legs and feet restless. If you could, you would stand right up, walk out that door, and just keep walking. Your mind's eye conjures mountains, trees, and lakes. You feel the wind on your face and hear the songs of birds high above. You breathe in deeply of that wild, clean air. An intense relief washes over you, and you catch yourself smiling. The urge is quelled as you resolve to get out hiking again as soon as you can spare the time. You wish you could go for longer, but you can't. You just can't.

I totally get it

It was three years ago when I finally embarked on my own sacred solo adventure. For years, I have felt an inexplicable urge to journey alone into the wild. I wanted the solitude. I wanted the challenge, excitement, and adventure. I wanted to be immersed in the amazing, expansive places I had seen in magazines and movies. I wanted to prove to myself that I could do it. I wanted to unleash my inner wild, the part of me that is primal and brave and free, and I wanted to see what she was really capable of.

No one gave me permission to go. I didn't have a sabbatical negotiated into my contract. I didn't get an advance on a book deal. I was an ordinary, 43-year-old woman, size 12. My mother lived with me, and I was engaged to be married. My best friend thought I was nuts. I had to make a choice. And that choice came with an uncertain outcome.

If you are reading this book, then my journey was for you as much as it was for me. I am certainly not the only one who feels a deep need for adventure. My sisters are all around me, women from every walk of life, yearning to throw off all that holds us back and run with wild abandon into the world's great beauty and joy. It pains me to see so many of us held captive by fear, guilt, stigma, and the multitude of other things that keep us stuck. I know you are stronger and more powerful than you can imagine, and I long to see you tap into that deep reservoir and discover the truth of who you really are.

I thought of you every day when I summoned the will to calm the panic and hike one more mysterious mile. I thought of you every night when I feared the wild things and chose to embrace them and learn from them. I did not feel brave and strong in every moment, but I thought about you and what you would need to see to overshadow your own dark places. And I held the vision of you in my mind as I willed myself to keep moving toward the light. You should know that I was weak, but together we were strong.

Chapter One

"You are the sky.

Everything else is just the weather."

—PEMA CHODRON

I meet Sophia for lunch at her favorite swank café on a shining afternoon in June. She had called earlier in the week, saying she could use a day in the sun. She arrives to the patio table wearing a bright yellow sundress and raspberry lipstick.

"Have you met someone?" I ask, as she tucks her skirt behind her knees and slides into her seat.

"I wish," she says, "If I had met someone, I would be having lunch with them instead of you." We laugh at the truth of this. Sophia has been waiting for her new prince charming and certainly would not have called *me* for lunch had he arrived.

1

"The pretty dress is for me then?" I raise my brows at her.

Sophia laughs, and then she sighs and shrugs. "Just trying something new," she says.

Sophia was more outdoorsy when I first met her. Her husband, Doug, was a rugged man and would play trail guide for her and their daughter, Isabella. They enjoyed many summer weekends camping and hiking and kayaking in the Shenandoah Mountains near their home. But Sophia stopped going out after the divorce. She always thought of herself as Jane to Doug's Tarzan, and without Tarzan... Well, it just wasn't the same.

She devoted herself to a different kind of adventure—raising her daughter as a single mother. She got creative with her work schedule and arranged after-school activities for Isabella. She took home projects she could complete after dinner. She volunteered for the PTA and for school field trips. She baked cookies for her daughter's dance recitals and cheered from the stands at every swim meet. Sophia has given her full attention to developing a bright, capable young girl and a meaningful career.

Our server fills the water glasses and hands us each a menu. He pulls a pen and notebook from the pocket of his long black smock as we browse the daily specials. Sophia orders the filet of sole with tangerine sauce. I opt for the Asian chicken salad, and our server nods in approval. He walks the order back to the kitchen.

Sophia puts her hands in her lap, sighs again, and looks off into the clouds. "Isabella is doing well for herself in college," she says. "She'll be a sophomore this year, and she's joined the tennis club."

"Awesome! She'll love that. I'm so glad she's staying active." My voice trails off. I still think of Isabella as a little girl. I shake my head. "It seems just yesterday we were splashing around together in the kiddie pool."

Sophia gets a wistful look in her eye. "I know, right? I remember Doug taking Isabella and me on this hike when she was seven. We worked our way through a thicket and emerged into a meadow brimming with wildflowers. Her face just lit up. She gasped, and then she giggled as we ran out into the meadow. We chased each other, and Isabella spun herself around and around until she collapsed. We lay down next to her on that carpet of wildflowers and watched the clouds go by overhead. We never stopped smiling. I wish I could keep her just like she was that day. She was so sweet and innocent, and she made our world feel magical."

The sun breaks from behind a line of feathery clouds. The rays grace her face, and a breeze lifts the ruffle on the neckline of Sophia's dress. She brushes a strand of hair away from her eyes. I see sweet Isabella in her.

Sophia comes back from her wonderland story. "It's been three years since the divorce and probably five years since I've done any hiking. I miss it. I miss the trees. I miss the crunch of the leaves under my feet. I miss the birds singing in the day and the crickets singing at night. Being out in nature comforts me, and I feel connected. I want to get out there again. I need to get out there again."

"Nature is good for the soul," I say.

"It's more than just that," says Sophia. "I feel like I've really lost myself. What happened to me? I had big dreams of grand adventure. I wanted to hike from rim to rim in the

3

Grand Canyon. I wanted to see the Northern Lights and kayak Glacier Bay. I thought Doug and I would do these things together. But he's gone. The divorce crushed my spirit and my dreams. I didn't think I could do these things on my own. I didn't *want* to do them on my own. I put my life on hold, waiting for my next great love. But there is no next great love for me yet. I don't know when, or even if there will be another guy like that in my life.

"I can't just sit around and wait anymore. I have this crazy urge to just go, just get out and do all the things I have been dreaming about doing. I have been thinking about this for several weeks now. I get butterflies when I think about the possibilities. I actually smile to myself, and this wonderful wave of peace passes over me. I think, 'Wouldn't it be awesome to finally scuba dive in the Biscayne Bay?' My mind soars in expectation. Then I come crashing back to reality, and I feel angry and frustrated. I don't think I can take it anymore. I'm not getting any younger, you know.

"But I also worry about what could go wrong. I keep going round and round in my head. Is this smart? Can I actually do it? What if I get out there and freak out?"

I am nodding in agreement. "Why don't you just invite Isabella?" I ask.

"I could, and we have taken some amazing trips together. We have made some really wonderful memories. But I feel like I have to do this alone now. I know it sounds crazy to most people, and I don't know why, but I keep thinking I need to go solo. I mean, you did it. Anyway, I just can't get it out of my head.

"I will be 48 years old this fall. I feel like I have been timid for too long. I don't want to let fear hold me back. I don't want to be contained by my worry.

"And about Isabella... I want to be a good role model. I'm not just living for myself. What kind of example am I setting for my daughter?"

I hear the angst in Sophia's voice. She is really serious about this. Our dishes arrive, with the flash of a smile from our server. "Fresh cracked pepper?"

"I'd love some," I reply. I'm searching for the right thing to say to my friend as the server turns the pepper grinder over my salad. Sophia is a strong woman, and she has made very smart, conscientious decisions for her life and her daughter.

"You have been an amazing mother," I say. "Isabella is a bright, capable girl, and that's because of you and the choices you made for her benefit. You gave her a safe, stable home. You were there for her, and you taught her how to be responsible and reliable. You did everything right, Sophia."

"I don't know," she says. "I tell Isabella that we don't give up in this family. I tell her that sometimes things are hard and life is scary, but that we are stronger than we think and that we should never let fear make decisions for us. I haven't exactly modeled that for her, have I? I was lonely, and I was afraid, and I gave up on my dreams."

"You shouldn't be so hard on yourself," I tell her.

Sophia pushes the fish around her plate. "The other thing is… Isabella is in college now. I don't want her to worry about me. I don't want to hold her back in any way. I want her to be able to live her own life and pursue her own dreams. I have to show her what that looks like. I want her to see how a strong, independent woman behaves." Sophia pauses, and she lets out a big, deep sigh.

"It isn't *all* about her, though. I also want to do this for myself. There are places I still want to go and things I want to see and do. I want to break out of my shell. I want to live a little. I want to be wild again. I want to prove to myself that I can do it. I want to show myself that I can go beyond my limitations."

I must say, I do love seeing some teeth in my sweet Sophia again. But I don't want her to get carried away. "You have nothing to prove," I tell her, "You *are* strong, and you are brave. You don't need to climb a mountain to be those things."

"I know," she says. "But I *want* to." A definite twinkle lights up her eye. "I think I would regret it if I didn't try. Who knows what I am capable of? I would always wonder, and I think I would always wish I had the guts to go for it. I don't want to look back with regret.

"And I can see myself doing it. I can see myself in the woods, walking a trail among the tall oak trees. I can hear the whispering wind and birds calling. I can feel the warm sun on my face. I can smell the bark and the moss. I can taste the spring water, and I can see myself cooking over the campfire. I can see myself in my tent under the stars. It's a totally different world out there. Everything is quiet, peaceful, and beautiful."

Sophia is back in wonderland, smiling like the vision of her seven-year-old Isabella lying on the lush carpet of wildflowers. "I just don't know where to start. It's a little overwhelming. I know I need to do some kind of research, but I don't know exactly what I'm looking for. I'm sure there's specific stuff you need to do to get prepared for something like this. I know I'm smart, and I could probably figure things out, but I'm a little scared I'll do something stupid without knowing it. I also know I need to get back in shape before I try to climb just any ole mountain," she says. And then she gets another little twinkle in her eye. "Who knows? Maybe I'll lose those ten pounds that have been pestering me," she grins at me. I can't help but grin back.

"I know you've been helping other women get out there like I want to. I don't really know how that all works, but I want in," she says with crazy confidence and such a beautiful spirit that I feel swept up in her cause.

"I've got you," I say. I smile all the way down to my toes because I know that Sophia is in for the adventure of her life, and the world will be a better place because of it.

Why go solo?

While it is fun to share travel experiences with others, there is something truly unique and special about solo travel. Studies show that the primary reasons women choose to travel alone include:

I am divorced or widowed, but I still want to live a full life.

I want to make my own agenda and schedule.

I want to visit family and friends.

I want to pursue a specific interest.

I want to visit an unusual destination.

I want to do some soul searching and connect with
    my deeper Self.

Chapter Two

"The wanting was a wilderness and I had to find my own way out of the woods. It took me four years, seven months, and three days to do it. I didn't know where I was going until I got there."

—CHERYL STRAYED

D o you see photos of beguiling, beautiful places and wish you could be there, too? Do you imagine yourself standing strong and brave on a secluded, breathtaking vista? Have you dreamed of bathing in a crystal-clear pool, a flowing, shimmering waterfall splashing down over your hair and shoulders? What is it about these images that call to us? Is it because these are carefree places? Maybe. We do not toil away in these lush gardens. That waterfall does not ring our cell phone and demand our effort. That mountain does not brood over our shoulder, asking us if we have finished our to-do list, chastising us when we don't, and making us wonder why we are never enough.

These are places that offer restoration and healing. These are places where we find our breath again. These are places where our heart can leave the race behind and discover its natural rhythm. These are places that draw us into unearthing the buried truth of ourselves, where we can finally discover that we are enough. And we long to know that we are enough. Deeply, powerfully enough. Just as we are.

Many women dismiss their yearnings for that sacred getaway. Our cultural conditioning has led us to believe that men go off on grand adventures, but not women. We are led to feel guilty for wanting something so extravagant for ourselves. We are led to believe that our place is in the cubicle and the kitchen and the nursery alone. We are led to believe that the world will stop turning without our constant care. We are led to believe that it is not smart, and it is not safe for us to go out there alone.

Every now and then we hear about a woman who seems to defy the culture, a woman who braves the great unknown and walks away with breathless tales. She has a certain something about her. We see her, and we wish we could be her, but a great many things keep us stuck right where we are. Resisting our deep inner urges, we often spend years vacillating, waiting and aching, afraid to go and afraid of not going. I was such a woman.

My past

I grew up an army brat. My father was often stationed overseas and would send home postcards from exotic places. He would send letters with photographs of himself in front of ancient structures. I was beguiled by these images and jealous that our family never got to travel with him. I dreamed of traveling the world one day, setting foot in the kinds of amazing places I saw my father in. My family was poor and did not vacation per se, but we camped a lot and took road trips to visit relatives all over the south. The most exciting trip I can remember was the day we visited the Carlsbad Caverns. I felt I had been in an important, mysterious place.

As a teenage girl, I read an article about Grandma Gatewood, the first woman to hike the entire 2,168 miles of the Appalachian Trail. She wore sneakers and carried an army blanket, a raincoat, a shower curtain, and a change of clothes in a homemade bag that she slung over her shoulder. She was 67 years old at the time, the mother of 11 children and the grandmother of 23. I was smitten by the idea of spending weeks alone in the woods, communing with nature and challenging myself physically and mentally.

In my 20s, I dated a world traveler. He showed me his pictures from Greece and Spain and talked of the grand adventures he had been on. He introduced me to hiking and kayaking. I learned that adventure is close by, not a world away, but that if you wanted to see the world, you could do that too. I desperately wanted to live that adventurous life.

You might have caught me in the coffee shop staring at the poster of the woman poised alone on the high mountain peak. You know the one I'm talking about. The shot comes from behind her. She is wearing a ponytail and a backpack, standing with her thumbs hitched into the straps at her chest, her shoulders relaxed and her gaze drifting over an expansive landscape of forest firs, purple peaks, blue sky, and winking sun. I might have been so deeply entranced that I could feel the breeze lifting my hair and the sun kissing my cheek. I might have absently taken a long, full breath, filling my lungs with the clean, wild air that seemed pregnant with possibility.

I met my husband-to-be, a handsome and passionate man. Rob had deep, probing eyes, a gentle face, and strong, broad shoulders. He dove headfirst into the ocean on our first date. He was enlisted in the Marine Corps and had spent time overseas. He talked of the beauty and intrigue of the Philippines and lamented that he had been stateside ever since. He talked of all the travel he wanted to do once he got out of the military. It was a whirlwind affair, and we were practically inseparable from the moment we met. I was pregnant with our son in less than two months. Cameron was our pride and joy.

My new reality

After Cameron was born, I went to work full time. I had dreams of making something big of myself. I desperately wanted to rise above the meager circumstances I had come from. I wanted to offer my son the kind of life I couldn't have. I wanted Cameron to have the kinds of opportunities I didn't, like studying abroad as a foreign exchange student. I wanted to teach my son that you really could do anything you set your mind to, no matter where you start from. I wanted to lead by example.

I put my nose to the grindstone and worked hard to advance. Balancing a career and caring for my family took all my attention and energy. I wasn't quite sure what I was doing, feeling overwhelmed and out of place so often, but I was determined to do it all right anyway. I was going to show the world what I was capable of. I was going to be the best professional I could be, and the best wife I could be, and the best mother I could be. Then, when I had done all that, I would deserve to have my dreams.

Our weekends were filled with household chores and homework instead of outdoor adventure. As the years went by, my dreams of exotic travel seemed a distant childhood fantasy. I told myself I just needed to grow up. I told myself that too many people were counting on me. At the same time, I devoured books like *Tales of a Female Nomad* and *The Hobbit*. I was inspired by the journey of Cheryl Strayed in *Wild* and yearned for a personal pilgrimage of my own. But I could never allow myself to do it. I wondered how on earth a person could just put their whole life on hold and hike through the mountains, carrying everything they would need on their back. It seemed impractical. It seemed impossible. But people do it every year. And the fact that they were doing it and I was not kept needling at me.

Eventually, my first stab at building the great American dream ended in a nightmare. Rob and I tore each other apart and made each other miserable. Our separation and divorce sent shockwaves through the ministry I was leading. My reputation was in question and my job was in jeopardy. Half the board believed a woman shouldn't be leading a ministry anyway. The very people I had sacrificed myself in service to spread vicious, hurtful rumors about me. My son dropped out of college after his first semester. Everything I had worked so hard to create was crumbling all around me, and I was working furiously to pick up the pieces and somehow glue them back together.

In the midst of this turmoil, another man came to my rescue. Edward Dudley, my middle school crush, had re-connected with me on Facebook. Edward was patient and understood the demands on me. He believed in my leadership and fiercely supported me. I felt heard and validated at a time when raising my voice seemed futile amid the clamor of enemies. We started dating long distance. He sent me flowers and love songs. He was goofy and sweet and tickled my funny bone. We did things like meet in Atlanta on a whim to see Tiesto live in concert. Edward rode in like a knight in shining armor, saddled on his great white horse, wielding his sword and whisking me up out of my flaming disaster. He gave me my smile back.

His father owned a winery in Washington. Pop wanted to expand, and Edward believed I had the skills to successfully launch that project. I flew to wine country to meet Pop and tour the grounds, the rolling hills, and row upon row of vines. It was like coming home, a love at first *smell*, with the aroma of fermenting grapes wafting through the winery. Pop was a jolly fellow who laughed with his eyes and gave warm, hearty bear hugs. We had dinner in front of the fireplace and sipped on the nectar of God. I was enchanted. I created my exit strategy and moved to the Pacific Northwest to join the family business in wine country. It was the stuff of Hallmark movies. Kind of.

The winery had bigger challenges than I realized, and I dove in headfirst to do all that I could to help. Once again, I found myself in a predictable pattern of working hard with high stakes and high standards. I devoted my days and nights to advancing the business. My relationship with Edward was still very long distance (he lived in Virginia), and I spent most of my time alone. My responsibilities and isolation threatened to derail my dreams of travel and exploration, again.

The set-up

The business started taking off, and my responsibilities grew to dizzying levels, but I made it all seem very easy. I was a private person thrust again into the very public eye, and it was important to maintain appearances. Edward and I got engaged, and we were being positioned to take over the family winery. I was bouncing around the state of Washington, hosting wine parties and art exhibits, and getting tagged in selfies with incredibly talented people. There were decadent meals and gourmet cheeses, and I was an expert at pairing them all with wine. It seemed to most that I had a dream lifestyle.

However, two very important things were happening deep inside that I couldn't tell anyone about. One, I was shouldering a workload that was totally unsustainable. I was busy from the moment my eyes popped open until the wee hours of the next morning, and yet we still couldn't seem to get ahead. The business was in a precarious financial state, and my personal financial security was tied to this ticking time bomb. Two, the industry was indulgent, and I was developing a very unhealthy relationship with alcohol.

Despite these challenges, my commitment to my work and loyalty to my family kept me from making any changes. I had invested too much, and too many people were counting on me. We had a ten-year plan. I didn't want to let them down. I didn't want to let myself down. I thought I could figure my way through it. I doubled down and worked even harder, faster, and longer. The dark circles deepened under my blood-shot eyes, and I wore my signature smile to distract people from noticing them.

I was no longer getting out into nature. I would drive through gorgeous mountains in the Snoqualmie Pass thinking only of the traffic and whether it was flowing. I would drive by the mighty Columbia River thinking only of my next appointment and hoping I would get there on time. The only adventure in my life by then was how to stay awake and dazzling from one event to the next. I hardly felt the inner ache anymore. I had too much to do.

The turning point

That summer, a series of events brought me to my knees. The talk around town was that I was marrying into the family business. I deeply resented this notion. I had come to the winery under the promise that I would never cost the company a dime, and I had made good on that promise. I always contributed more to the bottom line than what I brought home for myself. I felt like I was carrying the bulk of the workload, and it was affecting how I felt about my partners—who also happened to be my fiancé, his father, and my mom, three of the most beloved people in my life. My passion for the hospitality industry was waning, and I was having a hard time seeing how wine parties did anything to make a difference in the world. I missed having the kind of work that really mattered.

And then the unthinkable happened. I was arrested for DUI. It was a slap in the face. It was beyond humiliating.

Tolerance for my unhealthy situation had reached a crescendo, and now I had no choice but to face reality.

I knew my life had become unmanageable, and I knew I had to make drastic changes, but it felt impossible to extricate myself. The winery was woven into every fabric of my being and would be for the next ten years at least. To let go would radically alter my life and the lives of those who depended on me. I had no plan B. Instead, I kept my DUI a dirty little secret, and I battled intense shame as I continued my public façade and worked out my legal matters in private over the next few months. Looking back, I can clearly see just how crazy it was for me to believe that I could just clean up and keep up. But at the time, it simply felt like I had no other choice.

Eventually, I broke. It came on suddenly and with finality. I was done. I was done fighting for what was killing me. Every ounce of resolve to continue left me in an instant. Life as I knew it came to a screeching halt. There was no turning back. Just. Like. That.

Where do I go from here?

What do I do now? I had no idea. I did not trust myself to make any huge, life-altering decisions, given the extreme emotional state I was in. I needed to clear my head. I needed to process my pain. I needed to stop doing what I was *supposed* to do and start actually living. Once again, I was gripped with the deep inner urge to GO.

"It is easier to change my environment than it is to change myself." I don't know where I saw the quote, but I knew it to be

Truth making me an offer I could not refuse. The primal call of the Wild came to me again, and this time I answered.

That August, with very little planning and a lot of anxiety, I embarked on a solo journey that would take me from one corner of the country to the other, to the edge of myself and beyond. I packed my car as best I could figure, and with my nine-year-old pup as my only companion, I said goodbye to the life I knew and pressed down on the accelerator.

Chapter Three

"Strong women wear their pain like they do stilettos. No matter how much it hurts, all you see is the beauty of it."

—UNKNOWN

Was it necessary for me to reach a point of crisis? What if I had had the courage to take corrective action earlier, not just for my sake but for all of us? What if I had been able to take a step back and make the changes that I knew deep down needed to be made? What if I had been able to prioritize my own needs and actually heal? What might I have had to offer? Is it possible I could have prevented so much suffering?

Maybe, if I had been able to heed the cry of my Self and validate—with my actions—that her desires were important. Had my deep desire been to go to college and get my degree, I would have taken it more seriously. When my inner urge had been to homeschool my son, I gave it very serious

19

consideration. My deep inner urge for travel and adventure seemed foolish and frivolous compared to all the other things that vied for my attention (and my pocketbook). Thus, I diminished and dismissed it.

A mighty force that is repressed is dangerous. We can only hold it back for so long. The pressure eventually builds to a breaking point, and it will create a relief valve. A big, fat gaping one. This can be terribly destructive, damaging reputations, jeopardizing relationships, putting us at risk mentally, emotionally, physically, and spiritually.

I recently asked a group of women to describe their urge for solo trekking in the wild. Where in their bodies did they feel this urge, and what sensations did they experience? Here is what they told me:

I feel like I'm suffocating with racing thoughts.

My chest, hands, and feet feel tight, quick, and itchy.

I feel a crawling sensation, out of my own skin.

These sensations are remarkably similar to having a panic attack! Why is it that we cannot take our inner urging more seriously?

There is a reason you feel this deep longing. Deep desires are seeds that have been divinely planted for a purpose. They yearn in us to be cultivated, and they have powerful lessons to share. To *not* follow what is in your heart is to rob the world of your gifts. But I'm guessing you don't really see it that way. You feel noble in your sacrifice. You feel like you *are* giving your gifts, and you *are* serving with all of your heart. You don't know why you feel the urge to GO, and you certainly don't understand how that could possibly help the people you love. The very thought of it

20

feels terribly selfish. Your deep love for those who depend on you keeps your focus on what *they* need.

Feminine power

You see, we women are strong. We are strong enough to put the needs of others before our own. We are strong enough to bear up under the pressure of working full-time and running a household. We are strong enough to raise our children in a safe, stable home even when we ourselves are falling apart on the inside. We are strong enough to carry emotional burdens for the people we love, and suffer in silence about our own scars. We are the calming force in a crisis. We contain pain, diffusing its dangerous energy within our bodies and psyches. We hold, we envelop, we coax and nurture, and send forth faith. We kiss boo-boos and stroke egos and make a damn fine tuna noodle casserole, too.

My client, Trish, had this to say about the strength of women and the secret desire to venture out alone into the wild: "I believe that women are strong in so many ways, but we struggle to be acknowledged as strong. Our strength is more subtle and many times hidden. I believe there is a yearning to do something that demonstrates that strength physically. I read *Grandma Gatewood's Walk,* which I found very powerful. After surviving and escaping an abusive relationship and raising her children to adulthood, she walked the entire Appalachian Trail. I think when we suffer so much emotionally or physically in an invisible way, we yearn for some tangible way to show the world—and ourselves—how tough we really are."

Women have become unbalanced in our expression of

21

feminine energy. We understand our roles as givers and nurturers, and we believe that subjugating our own needs and desires makes us a better person. I have come to believe that we can be a powerful force for hope, healing, and transformation, and to do so does not require that we sacrifice ourselves. In fact, it is when we can validate and nurture our own deep Self that our light shines most brightly.

They say that you can't give what you don't have. So, how can we offer real compassion to others if we don't give it to our Self? Is it possible that our outward act of compassion is really a need to compel another to give compassion to us in return, to fill our own void? What would our compassion look like if it proceeded from a place of genuine power instead of need?

In this book, I am going to take you along my journey with me, sharing some of my private experiences and secrets I learned along the way. Each chapter has a Wisely Wild section, a synopsis of the most important life lessons I gleaned from that experience. And finally, each chapter includes a how-to section called 10,000 Miles in 10 Simple Steps, a roadmap for planning a sacred solo adventure of your own.

I am going to propose to you that we can, and should, embark on sacred solo travel in a way that is smart and safe. It can help you dive deep into the truth of your Self. It can bring you new passion and purpose. And it can lead you into loving deeper and stronger than you ever thought possible.

The benefits of solo travel

In the coming chapters, you will discover the hope, healing, and transformation available through sacred solo travel. You deserve to embrace all that your inner Self is long-ing for. Here is just a taste of the rewards of solo adventure:

- *"I can do this."* Experience a boost in confidence. You can find hidden reservoirs of strength within you that are yet untapped.
- *"I can rest without guilt."* Be nurtured by Nature. You can slow down, be spontaneous, and find your own unique rhythm.
- *"I can rely on myself."* Improve your problem-solving and decision-making skills. You can handle challenge on your own.
- *"I can make my own decisions."* De-prioritize the opinions of others. You can broaden your perspective, experience new things, and enjoy your own company.
- *"I am stronger than I think."* Challenge your insecurities. You can overcome fear by asking more of yourself than you thought possible.
- *"I am enough."* Absorb and reflect on your experiences more deeply. You can learn to sit comfortably inside uncomfortable emotions.
- *"I am connected to Earth."* Power is available to you. Growth happens in cycles. You can trust your instincts, adapt and adopt new behaviors that support you.
- *"I am connected to others."* People contribute to our landscape. You can open yourself to receive gifts and lessons from them.
- *"I am creative."* Manifest your dreams. You can find peace and create long-term health and happiness.

Chapter Four

*"Something very beautiful happens to people
when their world has fallen apart: a humility, a
nobility, a higher intelligence emerges at just the
point when our knees hit the floor."*

—MARIANNE WILLIAMSON

Never had I camped alone, but something inside me insisted I must do so. I realized at 40-something years old that I did not know my own deep Self. I had lived my whole life in the service of others, and yet I feared that my true purpose was eluding me. Despite my heroic efforts to build a worthwhile life, deep down I was not happy, and I was tired of repeating the same patterns. My instincts told me I could reach my deep Self, and maybe finally know her, by eliminating excess and returning to what was simple and primal. It was a sudden decision, but I knew I had to do this. I was afraid to go, but I could no longer resist the call of the Wild. My first solo jaunt would last five days.

Leaving it all behind—August 15, 2016

I am shaking with fury. I'm alone in my bedroom, hunched over the bureau, throwing a few articles of clothing into my red, roll-aboard suitcase, which is laid open at my feet. It is summer in Eastern Washington. The days are quite hot and the nights are quite cool, so I pull out tanks and shorts, along with long cotton pants and a fleece jacket from my dresser drawers. I toss in two changes of underclothes, matching the sets, of course. I roll my eyes at my matchy-match self. *Really, Sonya? I thought we were going primal.* But somehow the coordinated wardrobe helps me feel like I still have some semblance of order in my life.

Edward's college frat sweatshirt catches my eye and I pause. I adopted it early on in our long-distance relationship. I wore it when I missed him, when I was menstrual, when I was sick…it was my chocolate when I needed comforting. A fresh wave of grief washes over me, followed by an outbreak of goosebumps, as the reality of what I am getting ready to do really hits me. The thought of being separated like this is almost too painful to bear. I hold the nausea down with my hand on my stomach and close my eyes. I will bring the floppy grey top. I run my fingers over the red TKE on the chest. I lay it gently on top of the rest of my clothes, and I zip my suitcase closed.

I walk out onto the balcony, and my eyes glance over the neat, orderly rows of houses below. I pull up one of the camping chairs from its place on the concrete. I tuck it under my arm. I grab the handle of my suitcase and truck them out the front door and down the stairs to the parking lot. I lift open the back hatch of my Forester and load them inside. I return to the balcony and unlock the storage door. I fish around for my tent and sleeping bags, and I haul them downstairs too. The tent and bags have only been used once, a year ago, when I had convinced Edward to camp with me for the first time. This makes me angry. All those lost opportunities we were supposed to share together. I stare into the back of the car feeling a bit faint; then I close the hatch and return inside.

"Do you have toilet paper?" My mom is worried but wants to be helpful.

"No," I say.

"You will want toilet paper, Sonya," she says, and she hands me a roll she is already holding. I slide it over my thumb. I turn to walk away.

"Do you have a flashlight?" she asks.

"No," I say.

She rummages through a box in the laundry room and produces a flashlight and extra batteries.

I accept these too, figuring yes, a flashlight will probably be useful. I shake open a plastic grocery bag and drop them inside with the toilet paper. I round up the dog dish and a bag of kibble. I fill a small cooler with fruit and nuts. I fill a plastic gallon jug with water.

"Take this too," Mom says. She hands me a small black leather pouch.

"What is this?" I ask. I open the pouch and find a mini manicure kit. "Mom! I will not be doing my nails."

"No, but you might need the tweezers, and the little scissors might come in handy," she says meekly.

"Fine," I say. I toss it into the plastic bag with the flashlight and batteries and toilet paper, but I am accepting it for her benefit, not mine. I want to live on as little as possible. It's an important part of finding my primal Self.

"Do you have silverware?" Mom asks.

"No, Mom!" I take a deep breath. I want to avoid being hurtful. "Look, I don't want any silverware. I don't want a lot of stuff. I just want to go simple. Now that's enough," I say, trying not to sound too biting.

"How are you going to eat?" she asks.

"I am going to eat fruit and nuts," I say. "I don't need silverware for that."

Douglas Falls

I am shaking as I drive away. I am trying to keep my head about me, but I can hardly believe I am doing this. I decide on a campground two hours north; far enough to feel "away" and figure things out. I resolve to stay as long as I need.

I have no idea what to expect, even though I've read a detailed description of the campground. The words of that description are in English, but I have no frame of reference for them. What the heck is a *vault toilet*? What is a *pull thru*? I have only been camping twice in my adult life. I might as well be driving into a foreign country. My mind is playing games with me, telling me that I won't know what to do and I won't know how to take care of myself.

There is ample signage at the entrance to the camp-ground, which puts me a little more at ease. I read every word to be sure I am following all the rules. I can stay up to seven days. Quiet hours are between 10 pm and 6 am. Dogs are to be kept on a leash. Caution: Rattlesnakes. *Great.*

I drive around the entire grounds twice, inspecting each site and carefully weighing my options. Would I rather be close to the water or to the restrooms? Do I want to see my neighbors, or do I want to feel more secluded? *How would I know?* It is so hard to decide. It feels like the first time in my life I have only my own opinion to consider.

I choose a site that has a short stack of wood already piled next to the fire ring. I hadn't thought about a fire, but that would be nice. I whisper a thank you in my heart to the previous tenant for leaving it behind. I pull into the site and put the car in park. I turn off the engine and sit bewildered for a moment. *What do I do now?* I walk the dog.

I put Justice on her leash and take her for a walk. The sun is hot on my skin and the dirt is loose in my sandals. We walk by the RV parked at the site next to mine, and dogs bark from inside. There are two towels strung over a line and two camp chairs seated next to the fire ring. We continue around the dirt loop. The remaining five campsites are vacant.

I breathe deeply and try to quiet my mind. I still can't believe I am here. *What the hell are you doing here, Sonya?* Guilt and shame and fear wash over me. Tears well up in my eyes. What have I done?…What am I going to do? I am going to pitch my tent.

Raising a family-sized tent by yourself is no easy task. I don't even know how to describe it, other than to have you imagine a fishing pole bowing under the pull of a mighty swordfish. My tent body is looped onto that bowing fishing pole. Now imagine two more fishing poles, bowing. These three fishing poles are crossing each other from opposing sides of a triangle. Three swordfish are hooked and pulling at the same time. And you have to raise them all simultaneously. It takes me a solid hour in the heat of the day.

I take a step back and take a little pride in my work. I did it. I zip open the door and load in my sleeping bags and the long clothes I will wear for pajamas. I remember some detail from a meditation book I once read, and I position my bag with the head pointing north. I lay my gratitude rock next to the head. This is where I am sleeping tonight.

Okay, now what? Waterfall. I read about the waterfall in the campground description, but I haven't seen it yet. I reckon it's time to find it and cool down from my work.

Justice and I trace the dirt loop again and turn off on a trail leading into the trees. The temperature dips under the canopy of branches and leaves. Twigs snap under my sandals as we make our way down the path. I hear birds somewhere overhead.

I haven't seen any trail maps posted, and I'm nervous about getting too far into the woods with no clue as to the distance of this trail or whether it has any spurs I could get turned around chasing. But I have nowhere else to be. I have no schedule; no demands on me or my time. I take a deep breath and tell myself it will be okay. I am just following my feet and watching the little tail wag ahead of me.

I hear the laughter of children and the splashing of water in the distance. I put one foot in front of the other until we reach the falls. A clear pool stretches out in front of it and then narrows into a stream that continues deeper into the forest. A fallen tree offers me respite here. A small cairn sits atop the fallen tree, a sign from the universe that I am on the right path. I let that sink in. All of this feels terribly wrong and perfectly right all at the same time, but I choose to trust. I sit for a long time, and I breathe.

Darkness falls

I sit in my camp chair and stare into the fire as the sun sets behind the trees. Justice is in my lap, and I rake my fingers up and down in the scruff under her neck. The flames fight off the cool night air creeping in on us, and the darkness deepens beyond the circle cast by their dancing. I can't see more than 20 feet beyond. I listen to the crackle and the crickets, lost in it all, until all that is left is ruby ember.

There is no cell service and no Internet connection. I am completely out of touch with anyone who knows and loves me. There is no electronic entertainment to occupy or distract me. I am alone with my thoughts, and they start to play games with me.

I reach for the flashlight at my feet and click the power button. A faint circle shines briefly then dims to nothing. I click the button off and click it back on again. Nothing. I shake the flashlight, and the faint circle shines briefly before dimming back to nothing. *So much for having a flashlight.*

I peer into the dark in the direction of my tent, which is a good 20 feet away. I can make out the silhouette as my eyes adjust to the night. With the fire having gone out, it feels suddenly dangerous out here. *Do rattlesnakes come out at night?* I shudder at the thought. I shake the flashlight again and point the faint circle along the ground between me and my tent. It dims back to nothing.

31

"C'mon, Justice." The sound of my voice is stiff in the still night air. She jumps down from my lap, and I realize I haven't walked her tonight. I look around the dark campsite. It feels eerily quiet. *There is no way I am walking her now.* I decide she will just have to hit the bushes on our way to the tent, and I walk slowly enough to give her the chance. I decide I will have to hit the bushes too. *She would bark if something was out there, right? Yes, right. Nothing is out there, Sonya.*

I zip open the tent door, and it sounds disturbing and shrill in my ears. Justice hops inside ahead of me, and I zip us back in with a quickness. My heart is pounding. I feel utterly vulnerable. I need something to offer a sense of security in the gaping blackness. *Sleeping bag.* I unzip the bag and start to wiggle into the comforting cocoon when my mind calls, *Snake!* I yank my feet back out. I break out in goosebumps from head to toe. I poke at the bag. Nothing. I push around the bag, feeling for any kind of anomaly. Nothing. I start to wiggle back in again. *Spider!* OMG, seriously?!

I know my mind is playing games with me, and I know I can choose not to play. I take a deep breath and feel along the head of the bag, looking for my gratitude rock. I have been developing a serious gratitude practice for several weeks, ever since my DUI. My fingers reach the familiar stone and wrap themselves around it, bringing it to my heart. Justice is nesting at my feet, pawing at the fabric of the sleeping bag, spinning herself into heavy satisfaction.

The ground is hard and unforgiving beneath me, and I shift around to find a marginally comfortable position. I long for my pillow. I long for the streetlamp shining in my bedroom window. I long for Mom snoring in the room next to me. I long for the strong arms and cold feet that mean Edward is near. My aloneness presses in on me. I am grateful for the RV near enough to call a neighbor. I take another deep breath.

I look up into the mesh between me and the night. I squeeze my rock and begin giving thanks for all the good things that happened today. My mind calls them one by one, and I use this practice to calm my fear. My heart slows, but I can still feel its pulse in my temples and in my palm against the cold stone. I take another deep breath.

It would be hours before I finally fall asleep. In the still of the night, I can hear every sound of the forest. I fight the alarm in my heart by telling myself that Justice is sleeping soundly, and therefore all is well. A howl pierces the dark and sends shivers down my spine. *It sounds very far away, Sonya.* And then I wonder how a wolf howl might differ from that of a coyote. Some instinct tells me this one is coyote. I shiver again. I close my eyes and repeat the message that all is well. I am one with this world out here. I, too, am a child of the Wild.

On being Wisely Wild

- I learned that I could face overwhelming fears and move beyond them.
- I learned that I could manage my thoughts in fearful situations and tame them.
- I learned that I was stronger than I thought in every way—physically, mentally, emotionally, and spiritually.
- I learned that I was capable of figuring out the hard stuff.

- I gained an enormous amount of confidence in my Self.

Bring it back home:
How might these lessons apply
to other life challenges?

✺

10,000 MILES IN 10 SIMPLE STEPS:
The roadmap to your own sacred solo adventure

Step 1:

Name your fears and concerns. *Exactly what* is holding you back from the travel adventure you dream of? When I talk to women about their deep inner urge for solo adventure, they give me dozens of reasons why they can't possibly go. Things like their schedule and their responsibilities are clever disguises for what is happening at a deeper level. Keep digging. The root of every reason boils down to two things: fear and guilt.

The power of fear is the promise of something you dread. What is it that you dread? Is it losing the respect of your peers? Do you fear getting hurt? I challenge you to write down every worst-case scenario you can come up with. Let's get real and raw and name your fears.

Now, let's take a look at guilt. How does guilt keep you from taking the time you need for yourself? Does the little voice in your head say something like, "How could you do that?" The power of guilt is non-acceptance of Self. What parts of your Self are you unwilling to accept? Might you have wants and needs you consider unacceptable? Again, I challenge you to write these down in all of their ugly glory.

Sometimes our guilt and fears are legitimate. That is why I like to see these emotions as allies, not enemies. We can engage with them like consultants who might have useful information for us. That begins by looking them in the face and calling them by name.

Now that you have created your list of horribles, what do you do with it? Welcome to thought work and supervising your mind. My foundational work with my clients is to identify the thought patterns that are controlling their lives. The essential truth is that your thoughts produce your feelings, and you have 100 percent control over your thoughts. In order to challenge and perhaps change the way you feel, you have to work with the thought that is fueling that feeling. The good news is, you are 100 percent capable of overcoming whatever feelings are keeping you stuck, if that is truly what you want to do.

There are several models of thought work that could be useful to you. Simply Google "manage your thoughts" and find one that resonates with you. Another good starting point is the Ted Talk by Tim Ferriss on fear setting.

Scores of women are going solo. What might their thought patterns sound like?

Chapter Five

"I went to the woods because I wished to live deliberately, to front only the essential facts of life, and see if I could not learn what it had to teach, and not, when I came to die, discover that I had not lived."

—Henry David Thoreau

I took my second solo jaunt a couple of weeks later, buoyed by my experience at Douglas Falls. I wanted to build on what I had learned, and I felt I still had unfinished business. I had decided I could never return to the winery, but should I stay engaged to Edward? Who was I, really? What should I do with the rest of my life? In spite of these nagging questions, I was no longer full of angst. I had wrestled with my fury and released it.

What I struggled with on this second jaunt was guilt. I felt like I should be working hard, not goofing off. I worried I had wounded the people I cared about most. These thoughts plagued me, but I gently pushed them aside. I gave myself permission to take this time by reminding myself of all I had sacrificed in the past. The real question wasn't, *How could you do this?*, but, *Why would you not do this for yourself?* I had an opportunity to explore Mt. Rainier. I had an opportunity to discover my Self. I was *determined to relax* and allow myself to enjoy my time. I embraced my curiosity and spontaneity.

Sahara Creek Horse Camp—August 25

Sahara Creek Horse Camp is located just a few miles from the entrance to Mt. Rainier National Park in Elbe, Washington. I arrive on a Thursday in the early afternoon. Once again, I drive the entire grounds twice before choosing my site. There are many more occupants than there were at Douglas Falls, and most of them are in RVs hauling their prized horses. These powerful creatures are throughout the camp, being ridden, being brushed, and being fed.

A beautiful chestnut mare occupies one site, and I cannot take my eyes off her. She is attended by a solo female camper, as best I can tell. I feel an instant kinship, and I choose the site next to hers. I hear her whinny as I tie out Justice and pull my tent from the car. The smell of hay and animal fills the air, and I am in love with it.

The tent is raised and my camp set up in less than an hour. *I'm getting better at this already!* I pull a snack from my new picnic basket, a totally femme addition to my meager camping supplies. I spread my blue-checkered cloth over the picnic table and nosh on juicy orange wedges and cashews. The sun dapples through the tree branches overhead, and squirrels dart about, chirping at each other. I breathe it all in and settle into a peaceful ease. *Why would you not do this for yourself, Sonya?*

I would spend today at camp and enter the park early tomorrow. I roll out my bright yellow yoga mat and sit cross-legged in the center. I focus on my breath, and the scent of horses fills my nose and my heart. There is nothing for me to do here. No schedule for me to keep. No demands for my time or attention. All that is required of me right now is to breathe.

I begin a slow sway and allow my head to roll forward, then rock side to side. Breathe in. I wince at the crackling soundtrack in my neck, and then allow the weight of my head to gently pull the tension loose as I drop my chin to my chest and round my back. Breathe out. I slowly roll back up through each vertebra in my spine, finally sitting up straight and tall. I ground down through my sit bones and stretch the crown of my head toward the sky. I squeeze my shoulders upward to my ears on an inhale and loop them back and down again on an exhale. My breath fills and swirls in my belly, then returns itself to the atmosphere.

I lead myself through some gentle poses, remembering my favorite *Yoga with Adriene* videos. I love her mantra of "Find What Feels Good." Yes, this is the purpose of this long weekend of adventure—to find what feels good. I am not at all uptight about holding perfect shapes with my poses. I am using my breath to journey into my body and pause mindfully when something needs to loosen up. I continue stretching and breathing until I feel totally relaxed. I conclude my practice laid out in Savasana, the corpse pose of deep restoration. I drift asleep.

The evening is spent journaling and reading by the campfire as the sun lowers in the sky. Dinner is a pasta primavera lightly dressed in olive oil with fresh garden herbs and roasted vegetables. Justice and I take a flashlit walk around the grounds before bed. I crawl into my bag that night feeling totally at ease. My list is long for my gratitude rock. Classical music wafts from my neighbor's RV window. *I could get used to living like this.*

Mt. Rainier National Park

I rise with the sun the next morning, listening to the birds and squirrels and horses. The morning air is nippy, and I take Justice on several loops around the grounds to get the blood flowing before a breakfast of almond granola and a Honeycrisp apple. I've had a deeply restful night of solid sleep, and I can hardly wait to see the majestic mountain.

In the car, I tune the radio to the AM parks channel and listen to the informative briefs as I drive to the entrance. It will be a beautiful weekend, sunny and in the mid-70s. A young girl in pigtail braids under her khaki green ranger hat hands me a park map and newspaper at the gate. No fees this weekend, as the country celebrates the 100-year birthday of the National Parks Service. *Bonus!* I consider it a gift from the universe, another sign along this path that lets me know I am going the right way.

I find out Justice is not permitted on most of the park trails, so I will have to hike in the early morning hours while she stays kenneled in the car. I pull over at the first gorgeous overlook and, after closing my gaping jaw, open the map. I am astounded by the sheer size of the park. *Where do I even begin?* A giddy anticipation washes through me.

I drive the entire breadth of the southern region of the park this first day, from the Nisqually entrance through Paradise Valley to Stevens Canyon. I hike the Grove of the Patriarchs, a short and easy trek through a forest of towering red cedars, western hemlocks, and Douglas firs. The trail takes me over a suspension bridge and onto an island in the middle of the Ohanapecosh River. I marvel at the colors of the river rocks. I am dwarfed by the regal giants isolated on the island, some a thousand years old.

I come upon a massive fallen cedar and grow sad to see such a mighty warrior brought to the ground. I stand solemn for a long time. Fallen. The word feels like dead weight in my heart. Fallen. I notice a placard, walk to it, and begin reading about the fallen in the forest. I can hardly believe what I am reading. The fallen are just as vital as the standing. The dead, fallen trees serve as nurseries for new plant life. They serve as warehouses and even factories for essential nutrients that enrich the soil and foster new growth. They hold volumes of water, providing a reservoir of moisture that sustains growing trees in droughts. My sadness is lifted, my dim understanding illuminated. I am matured into deep respect for the circle of life and the ancient wisdom of mother earth. I had no idea.

Justice and I picnic as I browse the park map. I want to learn more. I want to deepen my understanding. I want to open myself and be matured. I choose hikes for the following days that would take me through the forest and meadow, along travertine streams and hot springs and glacier bodies, and to the face of the mighty mountain herself. I return the way I had come with an awe for natural laws I hadn't a clue existed. I am eager to be taught. I stop at every overlook and gaze into the beyond, wondering what secrets are held there. I breathe in the crisp, clean air and release every ounce of guilt for wanting adventure. I resolve to do more beautiful things like this for myself, to no longer deny the deep desires I feel from within. The student has found her teacher.

I return to camp long before dusk and build our fire long before it is necessary. Dinner is alpine cheese with hearty grain crackers and sweet, ripe cherries. I wave to Elizabeth, my neighbor, as she carries her camp chair under one arm and a covered dish in the other, joining another set of campers down the way. I watch two boys on bicycles making lazy laps around the dirt road. I write in my journal and read another chapter in *Walden* by Henry David Thoreau. I try to distinguish the songs of the evening air.

My eyes grow heavy as the sun sinks low, and I decide to follow in slumber. I dowse the campfire and take Justice on a final walk before zipping us into my tent and then into my sleeping bag. I gather my gratitude rock to my chest. My heart is filled with thanksgiving as I listen to the singing crickets and the snorting horses. I would be long asleep before the music plays from Elizabeth's RV this night.

I take on more challenging hikes over the next two days, pushing myself to go higher and farther, first with Rampart Ridge and then the Skyline Trail. I stress my body like this every morning and stretch it out with yoga every afternoon. I fuel myself with smaller, more frequent meals and drink a gallon of water each day.

I hear mysterious music in the trees as the breeze blows through. I smile easily and often. I nap. I watch the squirrels play and take photos of the daisies near my tent door.

I do all of this with no guilt. I work when I want to work,

and I rest when I want to rest. Nature is nurturing me, and I am healing. My body clock is re-setting itself in tune with the timing of nature's circadian rhythm. It is easy to rise in the morning and even easier to sleep soundly at night. *Why would you not do this for yourself, Sonya?*

I am meeting my deep Self and learning about how she operates naturally in the world. I am discovering how to feel my best. I am developing greater stamina. I feel energetic, happy, curious… amazing! I do not miss rich foods and fine wine. I do not miss late night movies and popcorn.

I really love being out in nature. I really like who I am out here. Turns out that I am the kind of person who eats simply and does yoga. I am the kind of person who smiles from the heart and waves at passers-by on the trail. I am the kind of person who climbs a mountain and makes angels in the snow. I can be the kind of person who keeps her promises to herself. I want to *be* this version of *me*. I resolve to figure out how to live as this person all the time.

On being Wisely Wild

- I learned that sometimes doing less is gaining more.
- I learned that the earth has an ancient wisdom that surpasses our understanding and ideas about how things are supposed to work.
- I learned that I could release guilt and reach for a new reality.
- I learned that I really like my deep Self, and this person deserves a voice and a place in my world beyond serving others.

- I gained a new perspective on what is valuable in life and what deserves my cultivation.

**Bring it back home:
How might these lessons apply
to other life challenges?**

10,000 MILES IN 10 SIMPLE STEPS:
The roadmap to your own sacred solo adventure

Step 2:

Cast a vision for your adventure. Why is this urge for solo travel calling to you? What do you hope to accomplish? What images come to mind when you dream about your solo journey? Again, this is deep work and the answers are not always obvious. We don't always understand why we feel this deep inner yearning.

Working with a coach can help you unearth what is hidden deep inside. However, you are fully capable of reaching this place without my help. I recommend baby steps. Assess your risk threshold. What is one small step you can take toward the dream that is in your imagination? Take that step. What comes up for you? What begs your attention? What doesn't? Write at least three pages, stream of consciousness. Do not filter.

What is the next small step you feel led to take? What can you do to boost your confidence and your resolve? What can you do to clarify your why? Take that step. As you take small steps toward your need, your desires will begin to reveal themselves to you. Pay attention to images, animals, and words that come to you. Take another small step. Trust the universe to meet you halfway.

Along the way, you will discover pieces of yourself that are being under-served and yearning for your attention. We want to enter into a dialog with this deep Self and ask her what she needs to come out of her shell. Does she need challenge? Does she need relaxation? Does she need creativity? Solitude? Take another small step in that direction. What comes up for you?

You want to set intentions based on these needs and cast a vision for your adventure that will serve these deep desires. You don't need total clarity to proceed, but you do need intention. Otherwise you are just on vacation, not a sacred journey. Don't get me wrong; a vacation is a wonderful way to recharge. But if what you seek is transformation, you will want to travel deeper.

Chapter Six

"You can do it! You've got this!"

—Encourage Mint

I took a third solo jaunt, off-roading to a secluded mountain lake in northern Idaho. The campground was two hours from the nearest town and was my biggest challenge to date. I returned more in love with nature and ever more certain that I had to dive deeper into her. Armed with a surge in self-confidence and a deep resolve to embrace my inner Self, I approached my closest loved ones, namely my mom and Edward, with the idea of what I would call my Walkabout.

Walkabout is traditionally undertaken by Aboriginal youth, who will venture out alone into the bush for as long as six months or more to make the transition to adulthood. While I am neither Aboriginal nor an adolescent, I desperately needed transformation. I would take the nomadic path. My goal was to seek out wild and primal places, to unplug from all that threatened to thwart my growth. I would drive into the great unknown and offer my spirit in communion.

Letting go—October 20

I have only the foggiest idea of how to prepare for an open-ended road trip of such epic proportions. My solo jaunts have taught me a lot, but this is so much bigger. *How much clothing should I take? How will I handle extreme changes in weather?* I take a few days for research and several more days of tedious preparation, but I know I'm still winging it. The urge to GO is nearly driving me mad. I give concerted effort to appreciating my time with Edward and Mom. I am nervous but anxious to finally get on the road. I have been working the car load like a Tetris champion, wanting everything just right, but impatience is starting to get the best of me. It's time.

Or so I thought. I hug my mom goodbye, and a panic ensnares me. *I'm not prepared for this.* My stomach erupts in furious fluttering bats and my fingers drain into icy tips. My heart pounds. *What if I get lost? What if I get hurt?* I move about the house in a rush, seeing everything I am leaving behind, and suddenly I *need* it all. I start grabbing this and that, thinking, "Oh my gosh, I might need a cutting board!" and "Oh my gosh, I might want my tambourine!" and so on. I am tossing random items in grocery bags like a mad woman, throwing them in the car, and backtracking for more.

The episode finally passes, about 20 sacks later. I take a deep breath and hold my mother tightly to me. I take Justice by the leash and walk us down the stairs. I open the car door, and she jumps inside. I pour myself into the driver's seat behind her. My heart is fluttering and my fingers are tingling. I manage to turn the key in the ignition. The engine roars. I take another deep breath, back out of the parking lot, and drive out of the neighborhood. I point my nose toward Portland and the Oregon Coast, an area my friends have raved about. I have never made time to visit myself. Until now. Now is my time. Time to see what I can do.

Bastendorf Beach, Oregon Coast

The mess in the back of my car keeps messing with my head. I have been four days on the road, and it is clear that I needed a better system for organizing my supplies. I am tired of digging around every time I need something. Life on the road is all about efficiency of time and space. I have figured out what I use most, and I want those things at my fingertips. I want the rest of it neatly out of my way.

I arrive on day five at Bastendorf Beach, where tent camping is permitted right on the shore. The day is calm and beautiful, and the overnight forecast calls for periods of light rain (a 55 percent chance). I scope out a site just beyond the dunes to avoid high tide, and I make camp. It's still early afternoon with plenty of daylight, feeling like a perfect opportunity to re-organize. I move all my belongings into the tent, including my laptop and my books. I spend three hours unpacking and re-packing, according to my new road wisdom. Like does not always belong with like. Frequency of use is the new codex. I'm delighted by my achievement and line my bags in a neat row around the perimeter of my tent. This is going to make my life soooo much easier.

My work behind me, Justice and I enjoy a barefoot walk on the beach at sunset. The scene is serene, the sky painted in pastels and the sun dipping behind the gently lapping waves. Victorian doctors used to prescribe sea air as a cure for all sorts of ailments. In traditional Chinese medicine, the water element is crucial to balancing the body and creating physical harmony. Modern research reveals that bodies of water can produce a mildly meditative state that can calm and connect us, increase innovation and insight, and even heal what's broken.

Reading by lantern in my tent this evening, I notice I have neglected to Velcro the rainfly to my tent poles. Today is the first time I have installed the rainfly, and I just shrug it off, remembering the forecast and feeling proud that I had actually been able to toss the fly up and over the massive tent by myself. The rainfly is tied down to the stakes, I reason, and that will be sufficient.

I snuggle down with Justice in my bag, fill my gratitude rock with joy and fall asleep smiling. I wake once in the dark to a light pattering on the vinyl above. The light rain has arrived. The sound is so lovely, and I fall asleep smiling again, so thankful to be here.

A new sound wakes me next. I feel disoriented. *What's going on?* It is still pitch black out, I can't see a thing, and a new kind of howling fills the air. Recognition floods my mind as I come fully into consciousness. The sky has erupted into a downpour, and it is the wind that is howling at me. *Oh no.* I have never camped in a storm before, and I have no idea how my tent will hold up. Anxiety grips me. My battery-powered lantern is still hanging from the loop overhead, and I jump up immediately, flail my hand above my head in hopes of running into it, find it finally, and click it on.

The tent sides are shaking under the force of the wind, the west side of my tent is bowing inward, and the rainfly is flapping violently. I imagine the wind ripping it right off, leaving all my belongings exposed to the rain. *Shoot! I have to Velcro that fly down!*

I throw on my raincoat and zip out the door of my tent. Justice runs out with me into the dark. *Shoot!* There is no way to control her right now. *I hope she stays close.* I wipe my hair out of my face and tuck it behind my ears under the hood of my jacket.

I still can't see a thing. I feel across my tent and run my hands along the guy-lines of my rainfly to the stakes below. The stakes are being tugged up slightly every time the wind catches the fly from below. I feel along the seams under the flapping fly and find a Velcro strip. I pull the fly down tight and wrap the Velcro strip around the tent pole. I move to the next and do the same, feeling my way to each one by one, around the tent body, until each strip of Velcro has been fastened down to its pole. *Now deal with the loose stakes.*

With the door zipped open, the wind is rushing into the tent and blowing out the body, lifting the roof up and sucking it back down. I feel for the guy-lines again, pull them taut, and shove the stakes back into the sand, one by one around the tent. I don't know if they will hold in this wind. The ground must be saturated by now. *What am I going to do? Think, Sonya. Think.*

I have bungee cords! I fly back into the light of the tent and tear open the bag that I think holds the bungee cords. I am hoping to secure the tent to something sturdier, like, a tree? I rummage through the bag but cannot find the cords. I pull everything out of the bag, and still no cords appear. *Where the hell are my bungees? What the hell am I going to do?*

I look around to figure out which bag is actually holding my bungee cords. I notice the wind is now blowing the west side of the tent into itself, literally. From inside, it looks like the tent is collapsing in half. I didn't know a tent could fold itself in half. I didn't know they are designed to do so during a major wind event. All I know is that my stuff is under there. I dive to the rescue under the bowing tent body, and I drag everything out to the east side of the tent.

The lantern rocks and falls from its loop above. I reach for it and pull it into my lap. Light is my only ally right now. The ceiling of the tent bends low and kisses my face under the power of the wind. My eyes grow wide at the sight of it, and I lean backward in horror, turning my cheek against it. It is crazy surreal, like the tent is trying to kiss me goodbye. Justice noses herself into my lap and under my hand, and I pet her, eyes wide, heart pounding. *It's just wind and rain, Sonya.* I try to calm myself so Justice will stay calm, too. I watch the heaving tent body, listen to the pouring rain, and wait for the storm to slow, praying.

Three hours later, the sun begins to rise and the wind retards, but there is no slack in the downpour. I have to consider breaking camp in the rain. My car is a good 50 feet from the campsite. I wrap my most vulnerable belongings into my sleeping bags, pull my raincoat back on, tuck my hair back under the hood, and make my first run for it, Justice on my heels.

The scene outside my tent is shocking. By now there are pools of standing water between me and my vehicle, and the ground is littered with tree branches. I slog my way to the car, passing a couple of campsites that are flooded entirely. Lower ground. *I'm glad I didn't pitch there.* I suddenly feel fortunate, in spite of my challenges.

I dash back and forth, splashing through the mud as fast as I can, emptying my tent back into my car as the rain continues. There is no Tetris master at work this time. I am mucking my way through the mud, throwing things into the back of my car with haphazard intention. It feels like the slow-motion drama from that bad dream where you can't go fast enough, playing out in living color.

Once empty, I seriously consider leaving the tent behind. That behemoth is going be a monster to get back in the car all drenched and muddy. Then a scene from *Between a Rock and a Hard Place* flashes to mind. Aron Ralston returns to camp to find his tent has been mauled by a bear and is floating in the lake. Being chased by this bear, he fishes his tent out of the water and fights back for his food. And here I am put out by mud? *No, Sonya. This is your moment of truth. Are you going to leave equipment behind because of a storm? Is this who you are?* I know that I will kick myself later if I don't salvage the tent. It is a dirty job, but I have to get it done.

The rain slows to a steady fall as I unlatch the rainfly, wind it up and shove it into the carry bag. I pull the tent poles from their corner sockets, and the tent collapses in a soggy heap. I feed the poles out of the loops, pull them apart at the connecting points, and fold them into their compact resting state. Then I feed them into the carry bag with the rainfly, being careful not to catch and rip the vinyl. The stakes pull up easily out of the ground, and I slip them into their pouch and slip the pouch into the carry bag.

I stare at the soggy heap of a tent, small puddles now forming in the folds and creases as the rain continues steadily down on me and my tent. *There is no way I can fold that down into the carry bag again ... I'll just have to roll it up as best I can and put it in the car... It's going to soak everything. Dangit! Think, Sonya. How can I collect the water and keep it from flooding the back of the car? I know! I'll roll it up into the dog kennel!*

I slog back to the car and pull the kennel out. Justice whimpers as I close her inside the vehicle and walk back to the tent, hauling the kennel. I unscrew the six bolts holding the top of the kennel to the bottom and remove the door. I nest the top into the bottom, laying the metal door between these pieces to avoid puncturing the tent. It makes a sturdy receptacle.

I pull one side of the tent over itself to fold it in half. The underside is caked with mud. The air trapped inside the tent causes the sides to spill outward. I grimace, knowing I will have to lay my body over the tent and into the mud to push the air out as I fold it over and over and roll it up into the size of the kennel. *Well, here we go.*

Another slow-motion scene plays out as I wiggle around in the muddy mess, pulling one filthy side over the other and using my body weight to push out the air. Once I have the right width, I roll my tent burrito-style and lift it into the kennel. A perfect fit. I lay the carry bag holding the poles and rainfly and stakes over my burrito, and hoist the kennel onto my hip. I carry it back to the car, hoping the kennel receptacle will contain the water and mud and keep the rest of my stuff relatively free from it.

I remove my raincoat and lay it over the tent burrito, and then I slide myself into the driver's seat. Justice jumps into my lap and licks my face. I let out a great sigh. *I did it.* I close my eyes and take a few deep breaths. I look into the rear-view mirror at the new messier mess in the back of my car. With my windshield fogging up and the smell of wet dog under my nose, I burst out laughing. *I did it!* I don't even care that my car is full of muck. I survived the storm. I'm going to treat myself to a hot latte and a dry motel room.

On being Wisely Wild

- I learned that I needed a better understanding of my equipment.
- I learned that trying to be perfect can make a bigger mess in the end than what I started with.
- I learned that I could rely on myself to handle unexpected challenges.
- I learned that I could laugh at myself and my situation, no matter how messy it was.
- I gained a new level of trust in my problem-solving and decision-making skills

Bring it back home:
How might these lessons apply
to other life challenges?

ᭅ

10,000 MILES IN 10 SIMPLE STEPS:
The roadmap to your own sacred solo adventure

Step 3:

Choose a destination and ideal dates for your adventure. Turns out, this was a soggy time of year for the entire West

Coast. While I could dry out most of my belongings in the motel that night, I was unable to open my tent to do the same. The rain would continue for another week, and I worried that I rescued my tent from the beach only to lose it to mold and mildew.

Deep inside, I wanted my journey to be a challenge. My experience in the storm on the beach served my vision for Walkabout—dive into primal nature and find out what you are made of. In this case, I was willing to take on whatever nature had to dish out. You may have other priorities.

Consider your vision from Step 2 as you choose your destination and dates. Is there some exotic place you have always wanted to visit? Is there a time of year when this area is best to be avoided? Dream your dream and do your research. The goal is to be Wisely Wild, not reckless.

Step 4:

Define your resource bank. This is where I work with my clients to develop a travel budget. These are the most basic decisions you need to make:

- Lodging: Will you be staying in hotels, with friends, or in state campgrounds?
- Food philosophy: Will you be eating out or preparing your own meals?
- Garment strategy: What type of clothing will you need? Are you visiting urban areas as well as wild places? Will you experience changes in climate during your travels?
- Transportation: What are the costs for fuel, airline

tickets, car rental, train, parking fees, etc. based on destination?

- Equipment and training: Is any specialized equipment or training needed?
- Entertainment: Will you indulge in entertainment, including visiting attractions?

We can draw up supply lists based on these decisions to determine what you might need to purchase or borrow. This is the most complicated and tedious part of the planning process, but I promise you that it makes a world of difference. You will want to do it well.

*I am happy to share my own insights and checklists, including useful resources to reduce your spending! I was able to take 10 weeks of Walkabout over 10,000 miles on only $2500. I offer one free strategy session to each of my readers. Email me to schedule yours at Sequoia1011@gmail.com.

Chapter Seven

"But let there be spaces in your togetherness and let the winds of the heavens dance between you. Love one another but make not a bond of love: let it rather be a moving sea between the shores of your souls."

—Khalil Gibran

Most of my conversations with other solo women on the road involve some discussion about the opinions of others. One of my first clients, Tiana, put it this way: "I'm an anomaly in my little world. Most everyone I know acts like I'm going on a death walk when I venture out alone." Sadly, this is an impediment to many who would love to take the leap into adventure. Let's arm ourselves with some facts, ladies.

- The average adventure traveler is not a 28-year-old male, but a 47-year-old female. And she wears a size 12.
- 75 percent of those who take cultural, adventure, or nature trips are women.

- There has been a 230 percent increase in the number of women-only travel companies in the past six years.

I know your relationships are important to you. That is part of what makes us being women so valuable. We *want* to safeguard the hearts of the people close to us. We go out of our way to make our loved ones feel secure. And so, we will be inclined to offer ample evidence for how common and safe solo travel has become, so we can put their minds at ease. Just understand that you may not be able to persuade your loved ones *at first*. You may have to make the leap and trust they will come around later.

Making the decision to travel alone means learning that it is okay to put your own needs and desires first. It is okay to let others own their feelings without your intervention. It is okay to have an opinion that is different and to act on that opinion without consent or approval. I know this will sound counter-intuitive, but taking a stand for yourself has the power to transform your relationships into a level of mutual respect that will have them cheering for you in the end.

My BFF

I have not told my best friend about my Walkabout, as I know she will try to discourage me. Cathy has a huge, caring heart, and she naturally worries about the well-being of the people she loves. I am fortunate to be one of them. I can hardly stand the thought of upsetting my closest friend since middle school. At the same time, I do not want her concern to influence my decision, and at this turning point in my life, I am putting the brakes on opposition. I want to surround myself with only positive energy.

I am barely into my journey when my Facebook posts clue Cathy in to what I am doing. Oh, she is livid. She sends me a private message:

10/20/2016 1:50AM

I'm extremely concerned what the heck is going on with you? When I mentioned that movie I was not trying to plant a seed for you to recreate it. What you're doing is extremely dangerous do you at least have some protection you're taking with you

4 animals if not other creepy people

I sigh heavily. The jig is up. Time to face my BFF. I take a deep breath and send my reply with all the love I have in my heart. I tell her she should know me better than that by now. I tell her that she does not need worry, and I remind her that my survival rate in challenging situations is 100 percent. This does not seem to help.

She proceeds to post a link on my timeline, a news story about a woman who had gone hiking in Oregon and went missing. She tags Edward in it, begging him to talk some sense into me. This is where I have to love her and love myself at the same time, drawing the line. I muster all the love and courage in my heart and send her this message:

> I need you to stop sending me negative energy.

 I was truly concerned for you after seeing that article and I wanted you to be aware of what was going on. This was only for your benefit. Im sorry.

> I understand, and I love you. Negative energy creates a negative reality. I am on this journey, concern or not. The best thing you can do for me is to think happy and positive thoughts. I have a long way to go, and I'm sure I will face challenges. That's part of life! But we don't need to create them using our own worrying minds. I am being very careful and smart. You should be proud of me!

I try to sleep in spite of my tingling tummy, hoping she can hear my message the way it is intended. I know it is possible that she will not, that she might get angry or offended. At the same time, I cannot subjugate the ache in my heart to her concerns. I cannot allow negative energy to be my bedmate. I hope she can understand that. If I need to ask forgiveness, I will, but I will not ask permission.

I rise the next morning to the crashing waves in Boiler Bay. The fog has rolled in, and a mystery is hovering on the ocean air. My mind is still troubled over my best friend, and I am trying to figure out a way to release the tension. I close my eyes and focus on the tiny droplets I can feel hanging on the breeze. *Let the heavens dance between us.* I take a deep breath. I get back in the car and continue south, windows down, Audible up. I'm listening to *Never Broken*, a memoir by Jewel.

Every few miles I see a bicyclist with packed saddle bags

on either side of their wheels. They wear white and yellow vests with fluorescent red triangles on their backs. They are cycling alone along the highway with all they need in those two saddle bags. Cycling the Pacific Coast is totally a thing—and I am seeing plenty of solo women doing it. *Huh! What I am doing is far less risky than that!* In fact, I have read about plenty of people who have attempted far more hazardous adventures. Jewel is one of them! What I am doing is actually pretty tame by comparison.

Mendocino—October 26

I release any further guilt over my little escapade and especially what others might think about it. I give thanks. Eventually, I find myself cruising along California Highway 1 into Mendocino. I recognize the name. This is the place my friend, Paige, spoke so fondly of.

I find the small coastal community of Mendocino delightful, full of little Mom & Pop shops, art galleries, and niche eateries. The town is dog-friendly, so I park downtown and wander on foot with Justice. I come across young backpackers on a café patio and enjoy their stories with a guitar serenade. I meet a travel writer and share a light conversation about shopping small and traveling with love in your heart.

Justice does not bark at anyone, just trots along with a smile. I do not feel like some strange phenomenon here. People don't act like I am on a death march. My travel goals are met with curiosity and support, not fear and criticism. Amazing how perspective can change so dramatically when you broaden your horizons.

I become calmer and more centered in myself with each step I take, and I let go of the need to prove I am doing the right thing. I discover a system of trails behind the visitor center that meander down to secluded beaches, and I wander those for a spell, barefoot with my toes in the sand. I immerse myself in the solitude and allow the sweet peace to wash over me. I sleep in a pullout a few miles away with an amazing view of the coastline, waves crashing in my ears all night long.

San Francisco & The Golden Gate Bridge

The next day, I continue south to San Francisco. My serenity is overtaken by excitement, as this is a place from my bucket list. I have always dreamed of visiting the Golden Gate Bridge. I have a fascination with bridges, and this visit seems particularly apropos. A bridge can be a symbol of life changes, crossing a path into new or strange territory.

I use BestParking.com to find free parking at Fort Point, a seacoast fortification under the southern end of the bridge. The view is spectacular, and I snap the epic selfie with the sweeping iconic structure behind and above me. It is a tower as much as a bridge from this perspective. I walk along the bay, watching pelicans fly and turtles swim. I twirl slowly with my arms out wide. I sit in the sun and listen to the lapping water and bask in the glory of a dream come true. She is every bit as majestic as I had imagined.

The Golden Gate Bridge is also a symbol of American ingenuity. It was said the San Francisco Bay could never be spanned by a suspension bridge surrounded by some of the harshest winds and climate conditions Mother Nature can unleash. And yet, here she is.

As am I, crossing into new and strange territory by myself. Mile after mile puts my past further and further behind me. I feel like I am coming into myself for the very first time. This work is about me and my soul, and I feel my deep Self coming near, feeling grateful that her voice is finally being heard; her little heart is finally being held and nurtured.

I know a mighty task still lies ahead, but I feel hopeful that the little girl deep inside will take my hand and we will forge a new alliance. We will make this journey together, and I will listen carefully to all she has to offer. I will no longer rely on intelligent logic and reason alone. I will learn to value input from my heart and from my gut, as well. I will no longer seek perfection in every action, but instead endeavor to be fully present in every moment.

On the other side

The exchange with my best friend proved to be a momentary hiccup, and we emerged with a closer and stronger bond than we had before. While she still worried about me, she followed my every move and gave me unwavering support. I let her know how much I appreciated her for being able to look beyond her own feelings and value mine, as well.

Putting my own needs first meant connecting with myself on a deeper level, too. After many years being shushed and silenced, my inner child finally felt seen and valued. She began to emerge in powerful ways, and I had a sense that she carried pieces of me that would one day become my wings.

On being Wisely Wild

- I learned that I could stand up for my desires and still communicate my love for others.
- I learned that I could do what others said could not or should not be done.
- I learned that I could deeply enjoy my own company, and that doing so made me a better companion to others.
- I learned to value emotion from my heart and instinct from my gut, not just logic from my head, when making important decisions.
- I gained a new sense of freedom in trusting my ability to direct my own life's choices.

Bring it back home:
How might these lessons apply
to other life challenges?

✿

10,000 MILES IN 10 SIMPLE STEPS:
The roadmap to your own sacred solo adventure

Step 5:

Reach out to family and friends. There are two parts to this equation: 1) Bring your mainstay support system on board with your plans, and 2) Arrange visits to friends and family along your route, if this fits your vision for your adventure. Respite with loved ones during your trip can be deeply restorative, especially if your journey is a lengthy one. Planned visits can also mitigate concerns from people who might otherwise object to your dreams of adventure.

The timing of this step can be important, so consider carefully. Should you reach out too early and be met with fear or criticism, you may waver in your resolve. You need to develop a firm commitment to yourself before you invite others into your dreams. Should your loved ones pose concerns, you will be equipped with information about your vision and preparations, which could go a long way in easing their minds.

Remember, this is your life and your choice. No one should rob you of your right to pursue what is within your heart. Be loving, be respectful, and be firm. You may find it beneficial to enlist the emotional support of a trusted mentor who can help you stand up for the little girl within who needs you just as much as your loved ones do.

Your cheering squad

I recommend recruiting a private cheering squad, whether you think you will need them or not. These are just a handful of people who you love and trust, and their only purpose is to support your journey. Include those who worry about you with agreement that only positive messages are exchanged. My prime communications strategy was a text group, where I could draft a single message, often with a photo, and blast it to my very important peeps. This kept my allies close, prevented sleepless nights, and minimized the time I would have spent sending multiple messages.

Chapter Eight

"Do the thing you fear most and the death of fear is certain."

—MARK TWAIN

Solo adventure travel can give us the opportunity to challenge our insecurities and face our fears. When we learn that we can rely on ourselves, we discover that we are stronger and smarter and braver than we ever imagined. Faced with an insurmountable obstacle, we can tap deep reservoirs and overcome what we thought was the impossible.

Yosemite Falls—October 27

Multiple people have recommended I take in Yosemite National Park. I am nervous about being alone in bear country. Actually, nervous is a serious understatement. I tell myself that I wanted a challenge, and this is my chance to face my fears. I know the possibility of being mauled by a bear is slim, as long as I am smart and follow the proper precautions. My head reminds me of all this, but my stomach still does somersaults.

What finally wins me over to Yosemite is the promise of multiple magnificent waterfalls, another fascination of mine. My brother Tyler shares my fascination, and he sends me a *Huffington Post* article on the "Nine most spectacular waterfall hikes in the West." He hopes he can visit them vicariously through me. Yosemite Falls is on the list. How can I let him down?

Before arriving in the park, I double-bag all of my food items in Ziploc baggies and seal them inside my cooler. I reckon this will be safe enough until I can get a bear canister. Nevertheless, I am going to store my food in my car and eat hastily when I need to. I shovel down some cashews and dried apricots, wash my hands twice and then apply sanitizer, making sure any remnant of the smell of food has been removed. Then I head for the entry, and I'm not turning back.

I choose the hike that leads to the top of Yosemite Falls. It is described as 3.8 miles, very strenuous, with 60 switchbacks, a 1000-foot climb over the last two miles, and spectacular, panoramic views of Yosemite Valley and the peaks beyond. It sounds like the perfect blend of challenge and reward. It is also a popular hike, a fact which I figure will reduce the chance of a scary bear encounter. I lift my hydro-pack onto my back, snuggle Justice into her kennel, lock up the car, and up I go.

It might be the fact that I have lived on fruit and nuts for the last few weeks. It might be the fact that I had only four-ish hours of sleep last night. I may have over-estimated my fitness level. Only halfway to the top, I start losing steam.

I plod along, putting one foot in front of the other, determined to make it to the top. I remember a bit of yoga wisdom from Adriene, how the energetic body can support the physical body. I focus on this, visualizing energy being drawn up from the earth via the soles of my feet and then coursing throughout my body. It buoys me for sure, but the effects are only temporary. I can't seem to sustain it. My pace slows to a crawl, and I stop for a break every several feet.

My head starts to swim, and I wish I had packed something to snack on. I had been too fearful of bear activity and had made a stupid mistake. I am terribly fatigued and I want to sit, but getting back up is too much of a struggle, so instead I bend over and rest with my hands on my knees from time to time.

I ask a hiker on descent how far it is to the top, and he says, "You're almost there!" I don't know if I should believe him. It strikes me as something they tell marathon runners to keep their head in the game. I guess it doesn't really matter. I am dead set on getting to the top, so I keep going, dragging one foot in front of the other.

At this point I am barely picking my feet up off the ground, and inevitably I trip. I fall forward and catch myself on the trunk of a fallen sequoia. I want to cry, and I squeeze my eyes shut to hold back the tears. *What am I doing? This is stupid. This is too hard.* "Help me, sister!" I beg out loud to snap myself out of that quit spiral. I visualize myself drawing energy from the wood via the palms of my hands. I am panting, so I focus on my breath until it returns to steady. I stand and carry on, little by little, inch by inch. *You don't have to go fast, Sonya. You just have to GO.*

It takes me three hours to reach the Top of the Falls. I arrive weak, lightheaded, and trembling, but I am elated. *I made it!* The final stretch of pathway is lined with large boulders, disappearing at the edge of the cliff. I make my way down the chute, and each rock is a like a spectator at the finish line, giving me a virtual high-five. The *Rocky* theme plays loud and proud in my head. Tears of relief well up in my eyes as I picture myself the champion. *I did it! I did it! Wait, wha???*

Instead of being at the end of the line, another trail marker points the way left to the overlook. I am totally bummed. I gather myself, straighten my shoulders and pick up my chin. *This* has to be the final stretch. I follow another chute of winding rocks. These lead to a spiral staircase of sorts, carved from stone, leading down and down. My favorite hiking proverb, "What goes down, must come up," warns me not to push too far, but I did not come all this way to give up now.

I follow the spiral stone staircase farther than I think is fair. And then I see it…. The outer safety railing ends, but the path continues. The only way to reach the overlook is to make my way along a rock ledge that hugs the mountainside. There is a grip rail affixed to the rock wall, but none to prevent a fall off it. And I am very, very afraid of heights.

Side note: I never feel *my fear of heights until I am up there. Then all the blood drains out through my feet and the involuntary shaking takes over. I have been very literally paralyzed by this irrational fear. I want to venture out there. I want to cross over. But it feels impossible. I retreat to solid ground.*

I am angry. I sit shaking and scared and seething. *This is a freaking national park! How can they make this so dangerous?!* I want to cry. I want to shout. I want to call Edward and share my distress with him. I want comfort. I want assistance. I want compassion. I want more than the only thing that was available to me—the utter edge of myself.

Should I stay or should I go? I gather myself and venture down to survey the situation again. Maybe it isn't as bad as it first seemed. I wind myself down the spiral stone staircase and face the end of the rail. I see a man in his 20s, stuck there just like I was. "Are you going to go?" I ask.

"I'm good," he tells me. His girlfriend has continued on without him and is standing on the platform below. He has no shame, perfectly happy to wait for her return. I peer out across the ledge again. I long for the courage to walk out there like she did. I long good and hard for it, but it escapes me. I retreat to solid ground.

I have now traveled down and up twice; my legs are trembling and my heart is racing. I decide I have pushed myself hard enough. I decide it is best to leave. But I can't. *How can I give up? I've made it this far. Can you really not go any farther, Sonya?*

I gather up my resolve and make another trip down the spiral stone staircase. This time I meet another solo female hiker, stuck the same at the disappearing rail. She has one arm hooked around the last bit of iron, leaning cautiously out for a selfie. We exchange reasons. She is also afraid of heights, and she has a daughter waiting for her at home. She says we are being wise and adds, "It's good to know your limits."

I retreat to solid ground. I agree. My name means *Wise Warrior*, after all. I tell myself I have nothing to prove. I tell myself I have reached the summit. I tell myself I am making the wise choice. But the image of that uncrossed ledge taunts me. Have I indeed reached my limit? Have I?? What if it is possible to summon the courage to cross over? Would it matter to me?

Somehow, that unventured territory is all that matters now. Once again, I make my way down the spiral stone staircase.

I meet a pair of female hikers making their way back up from the overlook. "I wish I had the guts to go," I say. I try not to sound defeated.

"It's not as bad as it looks," the woman on the tail assures me. "I am deathly afraid of heights, and I did okay. Just lean into the wall, and don't look down." They push past me and back up to solid ground.

I am now alone with my fear, and it swells within me and stares me down like the Leviathan. It is time for my final answer. Do I stay or do I go? This is my last chance.

I summon every ounce of courage I have in me, and then I dig deeper. I grip the rail. It is cold in my hands, and my shaking instantly intensifies. I grip harder and dig deeper. I lean into the rock face, and I do not look down. I inch my way forward, legs trembling and heart racing. I feel like I am holding on for dear life, and I pray I don't pass out from the fear. Or from the fact that I am no longer breathing. I grip. I inch. I conquer.

Once across, I realize it is not nearly as dangerous as I had imagined. I almost laugh at myself. My fear had made it seem insurmountable. But here I stand victorious, feeling like a warrior indeed. The view is ironically better from above, but what I see most clearly from this vantage point is the part of me that can conquer anything.

On being Wisely Wild

- I learned that I could challenge my insecurities and face my fears successfully.
- I learned that I could go beyond what I thought was possible, physically and mentally.

- I learned that I needed to take better care of myself, that sacrificing sleep and nourishment were not going to get me to the top.
- I learned that my mind would use others to validate a decision: those who stayed made it okay to stay, and those who went beyond gave me evidence that I could do it, too.
- I gained a deep respect for the needs of my body and its ability to perform under pressure.

Bring it back home:
How might these lessons apply
to other life challenges?

ᐺ

10,000 MILES IN 10 SIMPLE STEPS:
The roadmap to your own sacred solo adventure

Step 6:

Take preventative measures. "An ounce of prevention is worth a pound of cure." My number one recommendation to my clients who travel solo is a designated safety ally. This is a person who you trust implicitly, as they will serve as your life-line in case of an emergency. Ideally, this person is also your greatest cheerleader and source of support.

Before departure, be sure your safety ally is equipped with the information they will need to come to your rescue, should that ever be necessary. This includes the make and model of your vehicle, your license plate number and state of issue, your insurance contact and policy details, your blood type, and any emergency medical protocol.

As I would frequent wild places without access to cell service, I would touch base with my safety ally at regular intervals, providing my current location, my next destination, and my intended route. I used the freecampsites.net website to research my overnights, so I was able to text a screenshot of the campsite details, including GPS coordinates. We would agree on a time window for our next contact, and should I miss that by more than 24 hours, my safety ally would assume there was a problem and take action on my behalf.

Other important preventative measures include:

- Vehicle maintenance. Have your mechanic get your car in tip-top shape before you leave, and have a plan for maintenance needs on the road.
- Navigation. Have multiple options for finding your way. Do not rely on technology alone, as you never know when this might fail you, even in urban areas. A standard atlas is important, and more detailed regional roadmaps can be invaluable. National Geographic travel maps and AAA Triptiks are other useful tools.
- Health clearance. Get a checkup from your doctor and discuss your adventure goals. Have a plan for urgent care on the road and be sure you understand your insurance restrictions.
- Veterinary clearance. If you choose to bring your pet, meet with your vet to discuss where you will be traveling and what environmental risks they may be exposed to.

- Mental preparation. Keep your vision and adventure goals in front of you. Download podcasts, create an inspiring playlist, pack a couple of books or Audible selections to keep your travel mojo up. Know your limits. Do your research and get advice from people who have been to the places you are eyeing. If you feel like you are at the end of your rope, slow down and give yourself permission to reach out.

We take preventative measures so we can be *Wisely Wild*. Part of the lure of adventure is that the outcome is uncertain. No matter how much planning goes into our travel preparation, expect the unexpected. Are you ready to tackle the unknown?

Chapter Nine

"So the darkness shall be the light, and the
stillness the dancing."

—T.S. Eliot

I t has been said that it is always darkest just before the
dawn. After spending several weeks in primal places, I
can attest to the truth of this statement, literally as well
as figuratively. You would think after my triumph on Yosemite Falls I would have been walking on cloud nine, but this
was not the case. The challenge had depleted my resources in
every way. I was in a very dark place.

Back down Yosemite Falls

As I stand on the peak of my success, it starts to rain, making my descent as harrowing as my climb. The footing grows
treacherous rapidly, as much of the trail is carved of stone. The
constant drizzle creates a condition not unlike treading on a

freshly polished marble floor. I tweak my back in a slip early on and have to slow down dramatically, taking every step with gingerly caution, wincing in pain. I am hungry, thirsty, exhausted, and impatient to get back to the bottom.

About a mile down the trail my phone starts whistling with notifications. I have signal! I scope out a spot out under a tree, fairly shielded from the rain, where I can sit down and call Edward.

"Hellooo!" he says, in his signature, sing-song cheer.

"Hi, baby," I whimper. I am gasping for air and fighting back the tears.

"What's wrong?" he asks, and alarm deepens his voice.

"I'm just tired, baby. I'm so tired. I went on this hike that was harder than I thought and I didn't take any food and I drank all my water and now it's raining and I'm just so, so tired," I say, tears streaming down my cheeks. I fight to hold myself together.

"Sonya, I have never heard you like this. Are you sure you're okay?" he asks, his voice pitched with concern.

"I can't really talk, baby. I just needed to hear your voice. I need to get back to the car as soon as I can. The more it rains, the more slippery it gets. I'll be okay," I say, "I just needed to hear your voice."

"Call me back as soon as you can," he says. "I love you. Be very careful."

It takes me another hour and a half to reach my car. I am spent. Justice whimpers and jumps into my lap as I pour my soaking body behind the steering wheel. I wrap one arm around her and hold her close. I lay my other arm across the wheel, bury my face into the crook of my elbow, and collapse in racking sobs. I am so relieved to be back on my turf, back where

I can rest safely. Justice nuzzles her nose into my neck, and I let it all go. No need to be brave anymore.

I still need to make camp, and I need to eat. I also need to call Edward and let him know I have made it down. I drive an hour through the park to where my campsite will be located. I creep around the grounds, searching for a cell signal, but there is none to be had. Edward will be worried sick until I call him, so I turn out of the grounds and head toward town, checking my connection every several feet.

I drive through the tiny towns of Fish Camp, Sugar Pine, and Yosemite Forks, none of which offer any cell signal. I drive another hour south to Oakhurst and finally connect with Edward again, sitting in the Best Western parking lot. He is relieved and wants to know *what the heck happened.* I want to spill my guts, to tell him the whole story, to share the highs and the lows I have been through today, but I am running on sheer willpower, and that is wearing thinner by the second. I am desperate for food. Brain fog threatens to get the best of me. I choke out that I am okay, that I need to eat and get some sleep, and that I will call him in the morning.

Back at camp, I devour two cans of cold chowder and double-knot the empty cans in a plastic bag, my feeble attempt to avoid attracting a bear. Then I collapse in a heap in the back of my car and sleep for 12 hours.

Joshua Tree—October 31

Joshua Tree is located in Southern California, where the Mojave and the Colorado deserts meet. The park is best known for its namesake yucca, surreal geologic features, and dark night skies. The area is popular with rock-climbers, and the annual Night Sky Festival draws astronomers, scientists, artists, junior rangers, and enthusiasts from across the country to celebrate the night skies of Joshua Tree. I arrive on the tail end of this weekend, the dark skies punctuated by a new moon.

I see a coyote just beyond the park entrance. It is skinny and lollygagging across the roadway directly in front of my vehicle. It seems totally uninterested in my presence, and I am surprised to find myself more fascinated than fearful. Further into the park, the landscape is overtaken with intriguing stacks of irregular giant boulders. I take a run in the cool of the evening, stopping to view petroglyphs on the Barker Dam Trail.

I make my way out to camp before it is too dark to see. "Camp" is a wide-open swath of dirt, purported to be a dry lakebed about a mile square on land managed by the Bureau of Land Management, an agency that administers more than 247.3 million acres of public lands in the US. Headlights dot the area, owned by at least a half a dozen RVs and other vehicles, so I know I am not alone.

I crawl into my sleeping bag and fill my gratitude rock with thoughts from the day. I fall asleep quickly, with my glasses on, staring at a glittering display of brilliant stars, more than I ever imagined existed.

I wake a few hours later, thirsty, and after some restless tossing and turning I check the time. Only 3 am, and I am wide awake. I put my glasses back on so I can see the stars. The view takes my breath away.

I can see *into* the deep of space; light-years deeper than ever before. Fat, bright orbs, pinpoints of light by the millions, and dazzling dust have appeared and are now dancing before my eyes. I have never seen such splendor. Prominent and glorious floats Orion.

Orion

I have been mesmerized by the constellation of the hunter since I was ten years old, living in the rural town of Carnegie, Oklahoma. My favorite summer treat was to sleep outside on our trampoline, under the stars. Besides the big dipper, Orion was the only other constellation I could distinguish. I could easily find his belt, and the rest of the man would fall into place. I found his name magical…Orion.

The trampoline sat in the yard next to our shabby trailer and was the only evidence that we were not contemptibly poor. We wore thrift clothes, drank the expired milk my aunt gave us from the cafeteria, and scattered roaches with the flick of a light switch. I was teased by the girls who rode horses and wore makeup and legwarmers. But we had that trampoline.

Bouncing on the trampoline made me feel like I could fly. I would practice bouncing higher and higher until I got butterflies in my belly. It was here I got the guts to try a back flip, my first blind leap of faith. I could not see where I was turning, I had no idea how I would land, and I had no evidence I could accomplish this feat. But one day I tried. It was my first taste of victory over fear. I felt invincible, and I longed for more of that freedom.

Lying on that trampoline under the starry sky one night, I vowed to make something of myself. I would not be poor forever. I would do something important with my life. I would have nice things, and I would eat good food. I would travel the world and see amazing places. I pictured myself in Paris, wearing a little black dress and a wide-brimmed hat, sipping a latte in a swanky little outdoor café.

How far I had fallen from grace. I had run as fast and as far as I could from that sleepy little town, but I could not catch the stars. Deep down, I knew I was nothing. Oh I carried on a good show, but inside I was lost. I was deeply fearful of letting others see the real me. I was no longer connected to my people. I had let my family down. I had abandoned my friends and chased a silly fantasy. I drank too much and isolated myself from people who wanted to care about me. I had lived as a survivor for so long, and I had missed my purpose.

I filled my life with work and drew my worth from my achievements. This was far easier than opening my heart and being vulnerable. I could volunteer to fill the needs of others, but I could never let my needs be known. I felt like a little girl who had wandered into the big kids' class at school. I wanted to do school with the big kids, and so I pulled up my big girl britches and tried my very best. It seemed like no one noticed that I didn't belong here, and at first, I was proud of the ruse I had pulled off. But I thought if anyone could see the real me, they would just see a scared little girl.

Staring up at Orion now, in the deep, black indigo of the skies over Joshua Tree, I could see something that had been imperceptible before. I was astonished to find a nebula floating near his belt. Millions of tiny pinpoints of light in a milky swath could be seen so clearly. I was enchanted. I wanted to take a picture, but my camera phone could not capture it. I stared and stared hard, wishing and willing the sight to be emblazoned in my memory. I broke down in tears.

I was sitting under the most beautiful night sky I could ever remember, and I felt a world away from being beautiful myself. I lay awake all night with those tiny stars twinkling down on me, and I felt desolate and ashamed. *Where was my light? Did I have a light? How could I bring myself back from this very dark place?*

Oasis in the desert

As the sun rises, I ready my pack to hike into Lost Palms Oasis and Mastodon Peak, a little more than eight miles total. My soul feels as dry as that desert. I trek through shifting washes that fill my shoes with sand and tiny rock particles. I squeeze through a craggy ravine, scramble over mammoth granite, and climb down into a barren, remote canyon. It is dry, desert terrain painted with the faintest pinks and violets and turquoise sands. A raven calls from above, perched high, black, and menacing, against a pale orange precipice and blazing blue sky.

The Lost Palms are touted as an oasis in the desert, but no water is found today. Still, the palm trees sport their green fan fronds, the yucca grows tall and proud, and the desert cactus blooms. I see life in the wilderness, jackrabbits and lizards, resilient life that will not be defeated by an unforgiving sun. I feel such a life stirring in my own dry places. Maybe, just maybe, I can still bloom, too.

On being Wisely Wild

- I learned that our highest highs will often be followed by our lowest lows, and both will pass.

- I learned that the darkest nights offer deep perspective, revealing what was previously imperceptible.
- I learned that I could sit with uncomfortable and powerful emotions.
- I learned that life always finds a way, even in the harshest conditions.
- I gained a deeper understanding of grace and forgiveness, lights that shine in the darkness.

Bring it back home:
How might these lessons apply
to other life challenges?

❦

10,000 MILES IN 10 SIMPLE STEPS:
The roadmap to your own sacred solo adventure

Step 7:

Documenting and sharing your journey. You may want to capture your experience in the moment, recording what you think and feel in real and present tense. Your rearview mirror may not give you the full story, or you may choose to recall things differently than you actually experienced them.

You have many options, depending on your goals and comfort level. The most obvious choice is journaling, but even here you have multiple methods:

- Standard notebook paper with stream-of-consciousness writing
- A calendar/planner to document where you were on

any given day and a few short words to describe your state of mind
- A blank page notebook where you can include doodles and sketches as well as record your thoughts
- A guided travel journal with questions and activities related to your experience

Other great options:

- Scrapbooking
- A memory box to hold physical mementos
- A map on which you trace your route and write notes about what you experienced in each place

You may also consider sharing your journey. Exercise caution in posting live, for safety reasons. My personal rule is that I never talk about where I am or where I am going, only about where I have been. I would draft my posts and schedule them to publish at a later date, thus, my social sites were always about a week behind.

Several great options for this include:
- Social media sites like Facebook and Instagram
- Vlogging on YouTube
- A travel blog on Wordpress

Chapter Ten

*"The force that unites the elements
to become all things is Love; Love brings together
dissimilar elements into a unity, to become
a composite thing."*

—EMPEDOCLES

I arrive in Santa Fe on a rainy Friday evening. I am to meet an old high school friend at the Trading Post. While waiting, I browse the little shop, which is full of handcrafted, wearable works of incredible talent. There is a ton of turquoise jewelry here. I have been looking for a piece of turquoise jewelry for several months, a necklace in particular, to open my throat chakra.

My heart quickens with anticipation. There are so many unique designs here to choose from, I am sure I will find a suitable companion at last. I am in no hurry as I move from display to display, eyes wide and hopeful. I am fingering the necklaces and feeling for a pull from *the one*. And thus, I find it, as if by magic.

It is a necklace of heishe, small disc- and tube-shaped beads made of organic shells and polished stones that come from the Kewa Pueblo people of New Mexico, before the use of metals in jewelry by that people. A fossilized nautilus shell hangs from the strand, the tail of the pendant inlaid with turquoise. The piece is a collaboration between two artists, one of whom I have the pleasure to meet. It is an exquisite, one-of-a-kind piece of art with deep meaning. The shell forms a perfect representation of the logarithmic spiral.

The Logarithmic Spiral

I have been enchanted by the logarithmic spiral ever since a dream I had several months earlier. Unlike a standard spiral which circles back on itself in equidistant curves, the logarithmic spiral turns back on itself in increasing geometric progression, so that each loop spreads itself further from its origin, exponentially, and by mathematical precision.

Also called the growth spiral, it is a self-similar spiral curve that often occurs in many natural wonders. You can see the shape in cyclones, galaxies, flower patterns, and more.

The logarithmic spiral was first studied by Descartes in 1638. Jakob Bernoulli, a mathematician, was so fascinated by the spiral that he coined the phrase "eadem mutate resurgo" after it (translated "I shall arise the same though changed"). He left instructions to have the spiral and the phrase engraved on his tombstone when he died in 1705.

The logarithmic spiral symbolizes growth. Contrary to the perspective of our calendars, we do not live in a linear fashion. We do not grow by moving from point A to B to C in a straight line, leaving the past behind. Instead, life is cyclical, and we tend to repeat the same patterns and lessons over and over again... so much so that we often feel like we are just going around in circles, spinning our wheels. We get frustrated and angry with ourselves, thinking we should be beyond that by now.

But the reality is that important growth is happening through these cycles. We may have circled back around, but we are not in the exact same place. We have moved outward from our origin. And each time we circle back on ourselves, we have an opportunity to learn and grow exponentially. This is what the logarithmic spiral reminds me. *Was it merely coincidence that I would find such a treasure right here, right now?*

The Chihuahuan Desert—November 7

I have my heart set on re-visiting the Carlsbad Caverns during my time in New Mexico. The memory from my childhood still echoes in my head. It carries weight, significance. The temperatures will be mild over the stretch of days that lay ahead of me in the northern reaches of the Chihuahuan Desert. I will be able to take advantage of a cluster of unique attractions in the area.

Valley of Fires

I drive into the Valley of Fires first. The desolate park in the Tularosa Basin was named for the lava that flowed from a fissure in the earth's crust and devoured everything in its tracks. As the basalt lava cooled, it twisted and buckled into a gnarly flow that can be up to 165 feet thick and covers 45 miles of arid land.

I decide on a morning run, surrounded by the lava field and immersed in the sound of my pounding breath. It is an odd, grim, barren environment—thick, black carpet of hardened basalt, minimal vegetation of yucca and cactus. It feels other-worldly, as though I have landed on another planet. The sky is clear and the sun fiery. I can feel the heat on my skin. I can feel the heat in my throat on every inhale.

I keep an easy pace, a space-walk of sorts, noticing nuance in the lava carpets. This one looks like a huge bubble burst, forming a cave where bats take shelter. This one looks like a giant shoe print. This one has many folds and creases upon one another, as though the flow backed up against some stationary object and hardened there in place. I slow to a walk and move in for a closer look. I hike out over that lava and marvel at its coarse shaping, its imposing, harsh reality. And yet, somehow it supports life. Things grow in it. The plants and animals have adapted. Life always adapts itself to its environment.

White Sands Monument

From here, I sweep through White Sands Monument. Wind-blown dunes of gypsum span 275 square miles, making it the largest gypsum dune field in the world. Interesting sand formations rise and fall from the blowing wind, and the monument is known for its amazing sunsets.

I am delighted to learn that pets are permitted on the trails, and I pack extra water and snacks for us. I choose the Alkali Flat

Trail, a strenuous five-mile loop, which is absolutely, definitely *not* flat. The warnings are dire: Go only if you are prepared. Do not hike between the hours of 10 am and 2 pm. Hike with your cell phone OFF—it could save your life. If you can't see the next marker, turn around. Do not trust your footprints to guide you, as they can disappear quickly.

We are fortunate with the cooler climate, about 70 degrees. I head out toward the first maker. To my left, children are coming down the dunes on sleds. I chuckle at the playful sight. By the third marker, we are on the trail alone. It hardly seems like a trail, though. I am immersed in a sea of rolling sand, spreading out as far as I can see. I wonder if this is how being alone in the desert would feel like, and how one might feel being lost out in such isolation. I follow the path-full of footprints before me, leading me to the next marker. Then I notice one lone, barefoot set of tracks. These tracks are going the same direction, but they move off the beaten path just a few feet to the right. Well, Sonya? Are you going to follow everyone else? Or are you going to blaze your own trail?

I bend down and take my shoes off. The gypsum grain feels surprisingly cool and soft and not like sand at all. The stark white granules feel like powder as I walk barefoot up and over and across the dunes. I am sure to follow the posted route markers, but I am establishing a new, fresh set of my own tracks. I am going the right way and making my own way at the very same time.

The hike is glorious! Incredible! I am brought to tears by how magnificent it is. The expanse looks like a gorgeous, white sand beach without the water. It stretches out as far as I can see, reaching out as far as my imagination. The wind blows the sand into dunes of all sizes. Waves are carved in some places, and other intriguing shapes I can't hope to describe in others. I think of how this place is never the same two days in a row, constantly shifting under the power of the wind.

My mind soars into the mighty blue sky above. The chorus of *Circle in the Sand* keeps circling in me. A peace comes over me, and I cannot help but smile. I hike to a solitary dune and sit in contemplation. It is expansive, airy, and I feel light and expansive in myself. I linger for a very long time as the sun grows heavy in the sky.

Carlsbad Caverns

The following day, I creep into the belly of the earth in the Carlsbad Caverns. My lingering fear of the dark creeps into my belly as well. The absence of light hangs tangible about me like a black-out curtain. It is the middle of the week in the off-season, and the caverns are nearly empty. It is eerie, foreboding.

Small shines have been installed here and there to illuminate the towering shapes of the stalagmites. Water trickles over the rock and under my feet. I feel my chest tighten and my heart beat faster and weaker. I can hardly believe people first explored this place in the pitch black.

The caves are imposing, the limestone formations impressive. One looks like a totem pole carved with ancient images. One looks like a chiminea with fire in its belly. One reminds me of angel wings, curved in a protective cirque. One reminds me of a giant walrus. It is called the Rock of Ages.

One formation has the appearance of a pipe organ. Yes, I feel I have entered a cathedral of sorts, a holy place, a primal womb. The deep, brooding energy is palpable. A rush of awe and profound regard comes over me. I am hushed by it, as though noise would be forbidden in such a sacred space. I am besieged by an urge to reach out and touch the mineral face, to make contact with Mother Earth, to run my fingers along the wise wrinkles present there. But touching is not permitted. I keep my distance with my body, close my eyes, and draw nigh with my spirit. I am welcomed in.

Sitting Bull Falls

Justice is permitted to roam with me again at Sitting Bull Falls, part of the Lincoln National Forest. We enjoy a picnic together in the beautiful recreation area that was constructed by the Civilian Conservation Corps in 1940. The modest falls are fed by a spring in the canyon above, and water flows through a series of streams and pools before dropping 150 feet into the main pool area. It is refreshing to frolic in the green after my lengthy stint across the tawny, arid wilderness.

We hike up to the source springs before visiting the falls below. The vegetation is lush and varied with bushes and ferns and flowers of many colors. The gentle babble of the stream tickles my ears and my heart. We follow the trail about four miles up, around and back down to the pool beneath the modest flow of the waterfall.

The pool is cool and clear. The sounds of soft, falling water is soothing. The sun glints and glimmers on it all. A little fish swims by, and I say hello. I dip in the water, and in the washing feel reborn, renewed with clarity, all stress abated. I stretch out on the rock in the sun and allow my fingertips to dabble in the pool. Proverbial bathing. I am the nature child in all her innocence, purified.

The Fifth Element

It occurs to me that I have experienced the four primordial elements in succession: fire, air, earth, and water. I had not planned to do so. It just happened. It is another gift from the universe. Serendipity is leading me, teaching me, and I am an eager student.

I hear the words *the fifth element* in the recesses of my mind like a sacred whisper. I recall that kooky movie with Bruce Willis and Milla Jovovich. Didn't it turn out that love was the fifth element? I am anxious to find a coffee shop and do a little research.

The fifth element is known as *akasha*, quintessence, or ether. It is the intangible element that seems to hold all the others together. In Sanskrit, the word means "space" or "void." The fifth element is that which makes room for the existence of all else. It is the very first element in creation, and it is vibrational in nature. It is mysterious and pervasive, elusive and revered. This force was to become my mentor and constant companion.

On being Wisely Wild

- I learned that growth happens in cycles and to be patient and kind with myself in the process.
- I learned that no matter how dark the night, the sun always rises in the morning and can shed light on our experiences.
- I learned that nature can help harmonize these cycles

within us, leading us through the peaks and valleys and nurturing us along the way.

- I learned that there is a benevolent force that works on our behalf as we journey through life, delights in bestowing gifts, and communicates through nature and symbols.
- I gained access to a realm that is not easily explained or comprehended, but the more I pay attention, the more clearly I can discern it, and once tasted, its existence is undeniable.

Bring it back home:
How might these lessons apply
to other life challenges?

ᴡ

10,000 MILES IN 10 SIMPLE STEPS:
The roadmap to your own sacred solo adventure

Step 8:

Self-care and go with the flow on the road. In our modern society, we take the reins of our life and control our surroundings to minimize risk and optimize our experience. We set an alarm so we wake up in time to get the kids off to school and ourselves off to work. We sit at our desks and shove something in our mouths while we keep working. We multi-task with eight tabs open, a phone in our ear and a pen in our hand.

I recommend doing the opposite on your sacred solo adventure. We need to prioritize self-care and allow the list of "what needs to be done" to work itself out.

The most important rules you need to observe on this journey are:

- Getting adequate sleep
- Having nourishing meals
- Practicing healthy hygiene
- Adapting to what comes

I know, it looks super simple, right? But if you are anything like me, you will be more driven by what you can experience today and tempted to skip meals and shut eye in exchange for an exciting excursion. Don't make that mistake. Correcting course is not as easy as taking a stroll to your corner grocery mart or clicking off the lamp on your bedside table. You may have to go very far out of your way to solve the problem you have created, and put yourself in unnecessary danger.

My baby steps in camping taught me how my body wanted to operate to achieve its peak performance, and I put boundaries in place to ensure I followed its sage advice. We want to break those unhealthy patterns of neglect and use this time to adopt habits that nurture and nourish us.

Going with the flow is a mental/emotional form of self-care. It means accepting what is. It means loosening the reins and allowing ourselves to be flexible and adaptive to what is happening around us. I had my heart set on the Grand Canyon, for example, but it was too hot to hike leaving Justice in the car. I could have gotten all twisted up over this, but instead opened myself to other options and had an outcome I could not have planned any better myself.

Try opening yourself to unexpected experiences, not keeping your feet, not trying to control the outcome, and just see where you might be swept off to.

Chapter Eleven

"There is an invisible garment woven around us from our earliest years; it is made of the way we eat, the way we walk, the way we greet people."

—JEAN GIRAUDOUX

My first grandson was due to enter this world mid-December. He would be named Grayson, and I could hardly wait for his arrival. As the time for his birth drew near, I became convinced that I would eventually need to relocate to the East Coast. I want to be an active part of his life, not just a signature on his birthday card, in which I tuck a nice gift card because I have no idea what he is into and what he really wants.

Contemplating this potential move, I wanted to consider more than my new grandson. Edward's kids live in Virginia. I have family in Alabama and Virginia too, and seeing them more frequently is important to me. I decided to explore the

Carolinas, which would be centrally located between my heart-strings. My exploration led me into Brevard, a small mountain town at the mouth of the Pisgah National Forest.

Pisgah National Forest—December 1

The Pisgah is a temperate rainforest located in the Appalachian Mountains of western North Carolina. It is home to the first school of forestry in the United States and two of the first designated wilderness areas in the east. If I have to leave my beloved Pacific Northwestern paradise, this could be a close runner-up.

It is 29 degrees this early December morning. I am attempting to pitch my tent on a free campsite along Avery Creek. The written instructions tell me to camp only on the tent pads provided, which are comprised of compact gravel and dirt, and I am having the darndest time getting my tent stakes into the ground. I am using a rock to try to pound them in, but it is slow going, and my fingers are starting to tingle and turn numb in the sub-freezing climate.

A young man crawls out of the tent situated on the pad next door. I suspect I am solely responsible for waking him, as it is barely passed the quiet hour of 6 am. Guilt tries to toy with me. *I should have waited until later to put up my tent.* But I need my tent up now, and I don't always have to defer to someone else's needs. *I waited past the quiet hour, and that was sufficient.* I take a deep breath and release the guilt.

I expect him to be perturbed, maybe even grouchy. He is not. Instead, he says brightly, "That's quite a big tent. Do you need help?" I falter. I am used to doing things on my own. It proves that I am strong and capable. Besides, I don't want to put him out. I don't really *need* his help. However... I do appreciate the offer. His help would make the job go faster. And my hands are freezing, burning numb now. *I need to learn to accept the help I need.* I tell him, "Thank you, yes." And we go to work.

He wears a beanie on his head that is black with a white skull on one side. He wears the skull over his ear, so when he turns his head away, his skull is still looking at me. He has on dirty blue jeans, sneakers, and a wrinkled pullover. He has no coat on, and his hands are bare. I figure he must be a hardened camper or homeless. Turns out Chris is the latter.

I am not afraid of homeless folks. I spent nine years of my life trying to help them. Now Chris is helping me, and to thank him, I offer him a ride to town where he would access community services. He cleans up proper and puts on a black wool duster coat before climbing into my car. He thanks me, telling me that he usually has to walk an hour in the cold to get there. Then he leads me to a gas station where I can get a free cup of coffee along with my fill-up. I drop him off, thinking maybe I will see him at the fire ring tonight.

Asheville

I have read so many good things about this area. Travel-Channel.com named Asheville one of the Top 5 Pet Friendly Cities in the US. They are said to have an appreciation for the arts and a lively music scene. The WNC farmers market is open year-round. I am as anxious to explore this urban area as I am the forest I am camping in.

Justice and I picnic in the French Broad River Park and

walk along the water for a good couple of miles. We meet a perky male Chihuahua named Pepper, and the two pups romp around for a while. Pepper belongs to a bank professional, and his walker has been hired to exercise him every day. He finds out I am new in town, and he points me to his favorite places—the River Arts District just up the way, and the Highland Brewing Co., the first legal brewery in Asheville after prohibition. The Gaelic Ale is outstanding, as is the live music.

Afterward, I head to the heart of the downtown district and explore the city streets. I am delighted by the eclectic collection of Mom & Pop shops, and it seems every country's culinary genius can be sampled here. I follow the sun down an avenue and into the center of a silent protest at the Vance Memorial. Which is where I meet the poet, on the corner of Biltmore and Patton.

I see him out of the corner of my eye, seated cross-legged and quietly reading next to his baby blue, old school typewriter. I almost walk right by him, but the hand-drafted *Poet for Hire* sign catches my attention. I stop. *Poet for hire?* I take two steps back and lean around the passersby for a closer look. He seems not to notice me peering at him.

Curiosity walks me up to him and stands near. "What do you do as a poet for hire?" I ask.

He pulls the book from in front of his face and replies, "I write poetry on demand. People give me a topic, I ask a few questions, and then I write a freestyle poem for them. It usually takes me about five minutes." He is soft-spoken and mild-mannered.

I am intrigued. "And what is the fee for your service?" I ask.

He shrugs. "Whatever you feel it is worth. Most people give me between five and twenty dollars."

I squat to get a better look at him. Young. Clean. The paperback by Jack London. Clear eyes make direct contact with mine. Sleek and longish blonde hair spills from under his beanie cap. Thin goatee. Bare hands, though it is 40-ish degrees out. And that baby blue, old school typewriter—how fantastic is that?

He seems a genuine soul. I can't help but wonder what he would write about my Walkabout. So I hire him. I tell him I am on Walkabout. I started in Washington and I am now heading toward Florida. After that, who knows? So far I have driven nearly 10,000 miles.

He doesn't ask me any questions at all. He just observes me for a few moments. Then he starts tapping at the circular keys. I relish the repetitive clicka-clicka-clicka as he taps away, the type bars striking the ribbon against the platen in rhythm. He pushes the silver line space lever and continues at a steady clip, pausing briefly here and there, silently inquisitive. Once satisfied, he turns the platen knob, pulls out the page, and hands it to me. This is what he wrote:

a walkabout

> my footsteps continue to plunge
> into night mysterious,
> the dark folds adorned, with confidence
> increasing—from the west
> pointed east, as a sun whose
> already set—but marching trustfully
> towards a new light born east
> a new title, a lesson taught
> as exploring and extending landscape
> she finds parts of the map

once obscured by spilled ink - blank
met in listless trails, with a message
on tiring winter trees stirring a percussive silence sings,
to a heart with renewed vigor brings
a women on a walk about,
shedding that of winter and looking
towards spring

—phil krell

Songs of the Season

I learn of two interesting options to put me in the holiday
spirit this afternoon, a Christmas play at the community theater and a Baroque concerto to benefit a local animal shelter. I
believe the play will give me a better taste of the region's flavor.
"Snowbound" is described as a sweetly nostalgic slice of Western North Carolina country life in the mid-20th century. The
script is written by a local storyteller and features a children's
choir and a local bluegrass band playing new original music as
well as old Christmas favorites.

The theater is slam-packed with people, and I am instantly
overwhelmed by the crowd as I squeeze myself into the lob-
by. I make my way to the box office, rubbing more than a few
shoulders along the way. As I stand in line, I think twice about
staying. I haven't been around this many people all in one place
in quite a stretch. I check Google Maps for the distance to the
church, thinking maybe I'll go for the concerto after all and
wondering if I can make it in time.

Out of the blue appears a friendly, white-haired woman

who asks, "Have you purchased your ticket yet?" Her eyes are warm and benevolent.

"No," I say.

"I have an extra ticket, only one," she says. "I would like to give it to you, free, but you would have to sit with people you don't know."

"Well," I say, "I would be doing that anyway."

She smiles, and I smile. She hands me the ticket and leads the way. Suddenly, the crowd no longer feels so intimidating. The sea of people seems to part around us as I follow her to the door where her friends are waiting.

Sarah introduces herself, and her friends are Alice, Cindy, and Jeannette. They are lovely ladies, nicely coiffed for their afternoon at the theater. We enjoy chatting before the play and during the intermission. They are surprised to hear I have been on the road for so long and intrigued by the fact that I am traveling alone.

"How do you afford all that travel?" asks Sarah.

"It's not as expensive as you might think," I say.

"Where do you sleep?" Cindy asks.

"I camp," I say. "There are free campsites all across the country."

"Aren't you afraid?" Jeannette asks.

"I was at first," I say. "But I didn't want that to stop me. I figured out how to deal with the fear. The longer I did it, the less afraid I was. Then one day I realized the fear was just a story I was telling myself."

The ladies look at me in disbelief. "Well, maybe if I was younger," Sarah says.

"I met a 70-year-old woman when I stopped to see the

Marfa lights in Texas," I say. "She travels with her cat; walks him on a leash! It was the funniest, cutest thing. She had road maps from all fifty states in her car. We slept next to each other. Nice woman."

They invite me to dinner. I want to accept, but I feel like I have left Justice alone in the car long enough. I thank them, and we exchange email addresses and hugs. "Be sure to keep in touch," says Sarah. "I'll have you with me at another play if you decide to come back."

"I would like that very much," I say.

"If you change your mind, we will be at Rhubarb," says Sarah. "I hope to see you again."

Back at the car, Justice jumps into my lap and licks my face, her whole body wiggling with glee. "Did you miss me, baby girl?" I ask, laughing. I wrap one arm around her and scratch her chest. I turn over the key with the other, and we start back to camp.

The invitation to a nice dinner still hangs on my palate, and my picnic basket is suddenly less than inviting. Since I didn't pay for the theater ticket, I decide to treat myself to a proper bite somewhere close to camp. I find a local joint called the Phoenix, a farm-to-table restaurant touting live music daily.

I love the feel as I walk in. Cozy and warm with exposed red brick, a quiet dinner crowd, and a lounge seating area next to the woodstove. Local art hangs on the walls, and daily specials hang over the bar.

I salivate at today's special—Irish coffee, which I haven't had in ages. What could be better on a wintry night? I settle into a high-top and place my order, choosing a slice of strawberry cheesecake to complete my indulgence.

"Are you here alone, honey?" a woman seated at the corner of the bar calls over to me. She has long, blonde hair that falls in waves around her face. Her eyes are smiling at me.

"I am," I say.

"Would you like to join us?" she asks. The woman seated nearest to her has salt-and-pepper hair and square shoulders. The woman next to her is more curvaceous, with tanned skin and long, dark hair that falls straight down her back.

They are animated and joyful, celebrating the news from the Dakota Access Pipeline. Judy pulls out the chair next to her, and I slide myself in. Her friends are Carolyn and Keturah, owners of the Phoenix. They are all musicians.

"Where are you from?" Judy asks.

I shrug. "I'm on Walkabout," I say.

"Really?!" says Keturah. "We did that too!"

"Yep," says Carolyn. "We spent six months on the road distributing our last CD."

For the rest of the evening, we talk about music and travel and the challenges of being a small business owner. We talk about camping and hiking and the wisdom of the mountains. They call the chef out of the kitchen and ask for a kicked-up adult mac and cheese, and they share it with me. There is an easy likeability to them, and they love their community.

"How long are you in town?" Keturah asks. "Our band is playing this weekend. We'd love you to come."

"I wish I could," I say. "I'm going to be a grandma! I'll be leaving day after tomorrow. But I might be back. I am thinking about relocating, and I am really falling in love with this area."

"Well," says Carolyn, "the next time we play will be on New Year's Eve. It will be a big night. Some of our best local bands will be here. Good food, too. We'll give you any seat in the house."

"I just might take you up on that," I say.

On being Wisely Wild

- I learned that following my feet can take me on urban adventure too, and that can be fun and full of excitement in a different way.
- I learned that traveling solo does not mean you will, or must, always be alone.
- I learned that blessings come in when you least expect and often in surprising packages.
- I learned that I can best enjoy time with others when I am free to be myself.
- I gained genuine friendships with wonderful people leading unique and meaningful lives.

**Bring it back home:
How might these lessons apply
to other life challenges?**

꩜

10,000 MILES IN 10 SIMPLE STEPS:
The roadmap to your own sacred solo adventure

Step 9:

Meeting interesting people can be a fun and fulfilling part of solo travel. In fact, I think I get so many invitations because people see that I am by myself. I feel perfectly comfortable accepting or declining, depending on how I feel. My rule of thumb is to trust my gut.

If I have a sense of alarm, I simply decline and tell the stranger that I am meeting someone. This has only happened to me once. I have no idea why I would have felt uncomfortable, but I trusted my instincts and excused myself.

Otherwise, I have decided to enjoy the opportunities, and I have had plenty of them. I have shared coffee and campfires and deep conversations. I have been invited hiking and boating and flying. I have been offered homemade chili and sushi hand-drolls and fried egg sandwiches. Making that decision seemed to flip a switch, and people started feeling free to approach me and get to know me.

Meeting people from places other than your own backyard can broaden your perspective about a lot of things. A mindset that is widely accepted in Wichita might be totally out of the norm in San Francisco. A career path that is considered common in Dallas could be most unusual in Miami. You learn to meet difference with curiosity, instead of fear.

My favorite places for meeting interesting people are:

- Coffee shops
- Parks & recreation areas
- Campgrounds
- Museums
- Any guided tours

Chapter Twelve

"Perhaps grief is not about empty, but full.
The full breath of life that includes death.
The completeness, the cycles, the depth,
the richness, the process, the continuity
and the treasure of the moment that is gone
the second you are aware of it."

—ALYSIA REINER

Grayson was due any day, and I stayed in close contact with Cameron on Julia's progress as I contemplated when to make my way south. I knew these would be the last few days the two of them would have as a couple, and I didn't want to intrude on their last pieces of privacy. Every call from Cameron held expectant news, but one came as a complete surprise.

Sadness strikes—December 7

"Papa Bob is in the hospital," Cameron says. "He had a heart attack, and there were complications."

111

A knot grows in the pit of my stomach. Papa Bob is Cameron's grandfather on Rob's side. We had stayed with Papa Bob when we first moved to Florida. He was a quiet man who had a hard time showing his feelings, but he had welcomed us. He, along with his new wife, Kathy, had made room for us in their home. Family dynamics were hard to navigate, and after the divorce I had given up trying to fit in. Still, the news hits me hard.

"They don't think he's going to make it, Mom," says Cameron. "I thought you would want to know."

"Thank you, sweetheart," I say, swallowing hard as the saliva turns thick and bitter in my mouth. My stomach tingles, and it spreads through my arms. I remind myself to breathe. "How are you doing?" I ask.

He tells me about how visits to the hospital are hard, how everyone is on edge, and how he is doing his best not to upset anyone.

"I feel bad, Mom. What if he doesn't make it? It's hard to be happy about Grayson when Papa Bob is. ..." His voice trails off.

I don't know what to say. My heart is so heavy for him and for Julia. My heart is heavy for Rob, too. Although he is my ex-husband, we divorced amicably. I am wondering how he is dealing with this news about his father. I keep thinking about the rest of the family too, and what they must be going through. Relationships have been strained through the years, but they are good people, and I wonder how they are all holding up.

"I hear you, hun," is all I can manage as my mind swims. I should have something better to say. I should be better at this, for goodness sake. I am grateful he is sharing his heart with me, and I wish I could say or do something meaningful to help. But I'm just blank.

I lie awake all night wondering what I should do. Should I keep the experience of Papa Bob dying at an arm's distance from me? This is a family experience, a family that I am no longer a part of. I think about Grayson, and the real possibility that he will never know his grandfather. Tears well up in my eyes and softly spill down my cheeks.

Then it hits me. This family is my family. We share blood. These are my son's people, my grandson's people, and therefore, they are my people. Strange that I could ever see this struggle as separate from me. I need to enter this experience with my family. I need to feel and honor Papa Bob, to visit his spirit with my spirit, to send my love and light, and to feel the loss of him. We hardly knew him, but oh, did we know him. He opened his home to us when we needed a place to go. He was kind and generous and loving and wise. I have been wrong to keep myself separate. We share blood. We can never be separate.

Holmes Regional

"What are you doing here?" Becky asks me, shaking her head. Becky is Rob's sister, the eldest daughter, and her father is dying in the room behind her.

"I just thought it was right," I say. "We share blood."

"No, we don't," she says, still shaking her head. "You can't see him. He's too unstable."

"I understand," I say. My heart is breaking for her. She is careworn and beautiful at the same time, deep circles under her puffy eyes. She is obviously hanging on by a thread. "Can I get you anything?" I ask. "Do you need coffee? Something to eat?"

"No, I'm fine," she says. "I just need you to leave." She isn't mean, but she is insistent.

"Okay," I say. "I'm going to sit in the waiting room and wait for Kathy. I want her to know I'm here." I walk down the hall and out the double doors of the ICU.

I find a couple of chairs near the elevators, and a Gideon's Bible is laid on the table between them. I pick it up and run my fingers across the title on the cover. HOLY... I open to the Psalms and begin reading, tears welling up and spilling over again. I am praying the Psalms for Papa Bob.

I am grieving that Grayson would never know him. I am grieving that so much silence has filled the space between us. Was it wrong to give up on this family? Should I have kept trying to please them? We seemed so different from each other. But none of that seems to matter now. Papa Bob is dying. Would you spare him? I pray. Is it possible to bring him back to us?

Becky appears beside me, a look of contempt in her eyes. "What are you doing here?" she demands. I'm confused. Didn't we just have this conversation?

"I told you, I just thought it was the right thing to do. How could I not come, when I was so close by?" I say.

"This is not about you, Sonya," her voice is quaking and rising. "For once in your life, would you please not think about yourself! Would you please respect the wishes of this family! Now I asked you to leave."

I am stunned silent. A hot ball of tar fills my gut. The blood drains from my extremities and I feel dizzy. I'm not even welcome in the waiting room.

"Umm, okay," I squeak out. I stand, feeling like I am going

to faint. I bite my wavering lip and will the tears to halt themselves. "I'm so sorry," I say. Then I walk away.

"Good luck on your journey!" Becky hollers after me. "Have you found yourself yet?"

Papa Bob died the next day.

Vero Beach: New Life

"Julia's mom and sister are coming over this evening," says Cameron. "I thought you women should meet before you are all together in the delivery room."

My son has the most wonderful sense of humor, in which his wisdom shines.

I have been looking forward to spending more time with Julia and meeting her family, but now I am nervous. The ordeal in the hospital was unnerving, and I am second-guessing everything. Maybe I don't belong here after all. Maybe there is no space for a wandering soul. Maybe blood bond is just an outdated concept that no longer has a place in the real world.

Julia's mom, Stacey, and her sister, Jessica, bound into the apartment with arms full of items for baby Grayson's room. The house is filled with chatter as the ladies fawn over all things adorable and cute and precious. I feel a little jealous. They have been with Julia through the whole pregnancy, through every milestone, every scary moment, and every relief. There is nothing I can contribute now. There is nothing missing from the nursery, nothing needed by the time I got here.

Jessica has two boys already and plenty of advice for Julia, who is full of nerves. It is sweet to watch big sister with her little, lifting her chin and reassuring her with her matter-of-fact and knowing tone. I feel a pang that I don't have that kind of relationship with my own sisters.

Stacey is assessing the home and making sure all the final pieces are in place. She has an easy smile and bright eyes. She instantly warms to me and remarks how much Cameron has matured since the news about the baby. "We are very proud of him," she tells me. "He has come such a long way."

We sit around the coffee table, and they tell stories about meeting Cameron and his early dating bloopers. "Do you remember the time you..." and they laugh. It is obvious they love my boy as much as their girl, and I am grateful that he has found another good family to belong with. I am being welcomed into this circle, but I still feel like a stranger here. I've missed so much.

Later that night, when the house is quiet and it's just me and my son together on the couch, I reach for a shred of significance.

"Does Grayson have Christmas Eve pajamas yet?" I ask.

"No, he sure doesn't," said Cameron.

"I want to buy his Christmas Eve pajamas," I say.

Cameron smiles at me. Christmas Eve pajamas have been our family tradition since he was born. "Okay! That would be awesome," he says.

I smile and pat his shoulder. "You are going to be a wonderful father, Cameron. I am so very proud of you and all you have accomplished to get ready for your baby."

"Thanks, Mom," he says. "I love you. I'm so glad you are here."

"I love you, too, son," I say. "Thank you for having me."

Grayson Joel Morrison arrives on December 13th at 6:28 pm. Julia was a champ for a first-time momma, and her cheering squad may have gotten a little over-zealous. My son beams as he sees his little boy for the first time, and I watch him wipe a tear from his eye. I watch Cameron and Julia holding their baby boy together, filled with love and adoration. I am whisked back to the day my own son was born and the first time we held him, filled with awe and wonder. I wipe a tear from my own eye. The brand new baby boy is swaddled and suckled in the intimate moments after his birth, and I fade myself into the background.

The nurse enters and asks if it is alright to open the door. "Your guests are getting anxious," she says, grinning gently.

"Yeah, my phone is blowing up," says Jessica. She holds the screen up so Julia can see it, laughing and saying, "Grandpa is demanding to be let in."

Stacey helps Julia sit up in the bed, pulls her gown around her shoulders and situates the pillows behind her back, trying to make her comfortable. "Okay?" she asks. Julia nods, then she looks at Cameron.

"Are you ready, babe?" asks Cameron. Julia smiles and nods at him. "We're ready," he says to the nurse.

The nurse opens the door, and the waiting area spills into the room with the new son as the center of the universe. He is cuddled and coddled and kissed and passed from one adoring set of arms to another. He meets uncle and papa and auntie and bestie and the room is filled with jubilation. I am swept into the celebration. I feel like my heart could burst with the joy of it. I belong here. This is my new family, too. We share blood.

Finally, as the last visitors flow out of the room, my son walks to me holding my new precious grandson. He holds him out to me, cradling his head, and I gather him carefully into my arms. Grayson is smiling. Bone of my bone, and flesh of my flesh. I see flashes of Cameron overlaid in his bright eyes, and I smile back at him. I hold his face close to mine, and I say to him with syrupy sweet animation:

"I walked all day and night to find you. First, I traveled through the seven levels of the candy cane forest, past the sea of twirly-swirly gumdrops, and then, I walked through the Lincoln tunnel."

"Did you just quote Elf to him?" Cameron laughs.

"I did," I say, beaming back at him, unashamed.

Christmas

I spend the rest of the month in Vero Beach, catching up with old friends, getting to know my new family, cooking meals for the new parents, and singing to Grayson his father's favorite lullabies. It is magical, and for the first time since August, I long to have a place to call home again.

I rise early on Christmas morning and ride out to the beach for the sunrise, still wearing my messy hair but sporting new pajamas. I kick off my sandals and stroll the shoreline, sipping my coffee as the waves lap at my toes. Justice is at the end of her leash, avoiding the water at all costs but otherwise content to be near me.

A sparse crowd is gathering, and I walk a distance away from them. I sit myself down in the sand, and Justice climbs up into my lap, nosing my cheek to ask for a petting. I oblige, staring into the horizon at the coming glow. I lift my camera from its bag and loop the strap around my neck.

I made it. I crossed the country by myself. It was easier and harder than I thought. I had lost and I had gained, and it was all perfect. The sun rises and shines a beacon across the water. A flock of a dozen geese flies across the brilliant orange sky, calling out in harmony. A new day is dawning, and the possibilities are endless.

A new year and a new me too

I completed my Walkabout just before the first of the year. I traveled 10,641 miles in ten weeks. The need to dive deep with myself had been fulfilled. I had had the adventure of a lifetime, full of challenge and excitement, love and loss and healing. I was nurtured by nature and humbled by her wisdom. I experienced silence and solitude and a profound joy in my own company. My buried Self was unearthed and set free, and in this freedom was a new ability to deepen my relationships and to love harder and stronger than I ever thought possible.

Edward and I were reunited for the New Year's holiday. Curious about my experiences and wanting to share in the spirit of my new lifestyle, Edward booked a treehouse for us on Black Mountain. He has never been the outdoorsy type. The private, covered deck with a port-o-let, cell connection, and intermittent 3G service was his way of easing himself in. I was proud of him. After all, it was December in the mountains, and we would be sleeping outdoors. He wasn't brushing off my desires. He was trying to meet me halfway.

All of my relationships have an incredible new quality to them—they are real. I am letting the outside in and letting my insides out. I answer questions from my deep truth, people hear me, and I have so much more to give. I fill my cup, and my cup runs over. Welcome to my land of waterfalls.

119

On being Wisely Wild

- I learned that coming home is not always easy, especially when you have been deeply changed.
- I learned that not everyone can or will accept me, and that I can extend love and grace in the middle of conflict.
- I learned that I can hold onto myself while interacting with others.
- I learned that I have a place in the world, even if I don't feel I have much to contribute.
- I gained the freedom to be wild, the freedom to be vulnerable, and the freedom to be the real me.

Bring it back home:
How might these lessons apply
to other life challenges?

ᐯ

10,000 MILES IN 10 SIMPLE STEPS:
The roadmap to your own sacred solo adventure

Step 10:

Coming home gracefully. I found it incredibly difficult to come back home. I had begun living deeply and with freedom. It was hard to be inspired by the pressures of the work-a-day world. It was hard to relate to others still caught up in it, too. The old model of enlightened living was to run off and join a spiritual order and spend the rest of your days in solitude and meditation. Some are still called to this practice. I was not.

Integrating the things I learned into my life and my

relationships has taken a great deal of practice and patience.
Here are the hacks that have worked best for me:

- Incorporate 2–3 of your most meaningful rituals into your daily schedule. Start the day with your journal. Re-center yourself in the afternoon with yoga—I like Dragon's Breath. Keep the lights low in the evening, or better yet light candles, to signal transition to rest and maintain your natural circadian rhythm.
- Spend time outdoors every day. Take advantage of your front porch, back deck, public green and blue spaces. Ground yourself with the earth, close your eyes, and feel your connection with the natural world.
- Protect your boundaries. Practice speaking the deep truths of your heart. Don't expect others to understand or approve, but do it anyway. Offer grace where it is needed, especially with yourself. *Be* the compassionate person you need, and lead by example.
- Continue to exercise your instincts. Your heart and your gut are always offering information. Tune in and DO what you know to do.
- Find someone to share your journey with, someone who understands what you have experienced, who can support and encourage you, who can remind you who you really are. (*There are a number of social media groups for solo female travelers, and I would personally* **love** *to connect with you and hear your story. You can find me at Facebook.com/sequoia101–Sonya Louise. I am easily accessible on Facebook Messenger.*)
- Take regular excursions to renew, revive and honor your Wild , even if they are short.

Chapter Thirteen

"Well-behaved women seldom make history."

—Laurel Thatcher Ulrich

Women on walkabout

When I talk about my journey, women from all walks of life will secretly confide in me that they too dream of sacred solo travel. "I've always wanted to do what you are doing, but I could never actually go," they tell me. They say it almost under their breath, as though saying it out loud would be irresponsible. At first it made me curious. I would ask, "You know that you can totally do that, right? I mean, it is totally in your power to GO."

"Oh no, no," they would reply, "*not me.*"

This book is my way of saying, *Well why not?* You absolutely CAN. You absolutely can have freedom and wide-open spaces. You absolutely can have excitement and adventure in breathtaking scenery. You absolutely can have new passion and purpose. You can do all of this AND have deeper, more authentic relationships, loving harder and stronger than you ever thought possible. You have permission, and this is your roadmap.

Detours and warning signs

You are now equipped with all you need to experience your own solo travel adventure. You have what it takes to join the thousands of women who are taking the leap. You know that you can be Wisely Wild, and that sacred solo travel just might be the smartest thing you ever do for yourself and the people who love you. You have a step-by-step guide to lead you on your journey.

A few words of caution before you GO....

Fear will try to alarm you

I have a confession to make. While I am deeply drawn to wild places, I also harbor a secret fear of them. There are two primary reasons for this. First, the possibility of an animal encounter feels terribly dangerous to me. I did not grow up in the wilderness, and my understanding of animal behavior was informed by watching *"When Animals Attack"* on the Nature Channel. Steve Erwin tried to alleviate my fears as the Crocodile Hunter, but that only went so far. I know that with the proper training and mindset, animal encounters can be educational and even magical. My brain acknowledges this, but my belly still does somersaults when I venture out alone.

The second reason for my deep fear is that I have a legendary lack of direction. Even in familiar places, I can get turned around easily and end up lost. The running joke is asking me not, "How was the meeting?" but, "Did you make it to the meeting?" And I hang my head in shame more often than I'd like to admit. When lost, I can go into a full-on panic attack, unable to ask for direction because I can't speak or even breathe. And yet, here I am with an insane, relentless drive to venture out alone into the mountains.

I am totally, seriously the most unlikely person to take on solo hiking and road tripping.

I overcame these fears by making a choice to do so. When Cameron was young I taught him this mantra: *Fear is not my master; I am master over my fear.* I believe fear is a mindset that we can control, and I prove that to myself by facing fearful situations.

In the middle of my trepidation, I began to squeeze in solo day hikes. I researched popular trails near my home to take baby steps toward my goals. My intent was to get out once a month and learn the ropes. I often fell short of that target, but I saw many beautiful places, and my courage grew each step along the way. I came across more solo hikers than I expected, which further built up my confidence. I was proud of myself for what I could accomplish, and I learned powerful lessons doing it.

People call me brave. The funny thing is, I never considered myself very brave. I just want to live a life that matters, and taking steps toward my dream is less painful than being stuck just dreaming about it. I am also acutely aware that I am not just living for myself. My son is watching me (and now I have a grandson, too!), and if I want him to have the courage to chase his dreams, I need to set that example for him.

Your mind is programmed to repeat the same patterns and protect you from anything it deems too risky to your status quo. Even positive change can trigger danger signals in your brain, causing you to abort your best intentions. Consider the number of broken New Year's resolutions.

Anticipate a barrage of *what ifs* to try to torture you into submission. *What if I get lost? What if I get out there and freak out? What if I can't protect myself? What if my car breaks down? What if I run out of money? What if my mom needs me? What if my husband leaves me? What if I am not enough?*

Your mind will then likely manifest compromises or bribes to keep you from moving forward. A friend will be suddenly available to adventure with you. Look! You don't have to go alone after all! You'll be offered a promotion with new responsibilities and higher pay. Look! Your hard work is finally being rewarded!

Unless you have already mastered your mind and your thought life, you will likely be waylaid by misgivings and fabulous concessions. That's why it is most helpful to have an ally working with you, helping you explore the deeper meaning of your fears and assess what kind of corrective action is needed.

Stigma will try to bind you

Your friends and family will probably be all too eager to reinforce your doubts. They may tell you how very dangerous it is for a woman to travel alone. They may insinuate, or tell you outright, that you are being selfish for choosing to take time for what you need. It may be difficult to find anyone who believes in what you want to accomplish and in your ability to do so.

My clients often find me participating in women's adventure groups on Facebook. In a recent post, I asked, "Why do you think the movie *Wild* became so wildly popular? What is it about this story that resonates with so many women?" I was shocked at the commentary. Even among adventuring women, Cheryl Strayed's character was often described as selfish, arrogant, and irresponsible. I began probing, trying to understand where this sentiment was coming from. Then I received this private message from Natalie:

"What struck me was one woman's claim that Strayed was 'unsavory'. I very recently got divorced and have been thinking a lot about emotional labor (so your question is timely for me!). I found that after years of neglecting myself and doing the bulk of the emotional work in my marriage by myself—working through problems, setting goals, working toward joint goals, asking for and offering affection—I got fed up. I knew I was missing something, and while my self-hurt wasn't nearly as extreme as Strayed's, I certainly hadn't been treating myself with good care. I never made myself a priority in my marriage, nor did my ex prioritize me—so I was low on the list for everyone! I discovered when I put my foot down, set my boundaries and upheld them, and stated my expectations—something we all have not just the right, but the OBLIGATION, to do in our own lives—I was met with pushback from all over. Interestingly, my ex was never cross-examined; no one raised a brow and asked him, "Well why didn't you take your wife's 10,000 pleas for change seriously?""

I got the distinct impression that I was seen as self-interested (which evidently is bad?) and uncaring (which is the opposite of true: I had cared so much, for so long, that I just couldn't sustain it at that level anymore).

So I'm left with questions:

- Why are women often the ones left holding the emotional bag?
- Why are we discouraged from asking for help?
- Why are we deemed selfish for prioritizing ourselves and demanding time and space to work through our problems, determine our needs, and insisting that we are worthy of the lives we want?
- Why are our boundaries 'okay' to violate repeatedly, yet, it's not okay when we enforce them?
- Why are we not allowed to offer ourselves the same leniency and forgiveness we are implicitly directed to offer others?
- Why are we the bad guy when we do the exact same thing men do?

In the case of *Wild,* if a man's troubled childhood and complicated grief led him to make a series of poor choices and neglect his marriage—and he decided to go off and figure things out, treating his wife with as much respect as he could conjure up in his broken state—would we call him unsavory? Or would he be a sympathetic character?"

Unfortunately, our social norms charge women with being the caretakers of the world, but do not permit us to be caretakers of ourselves. Without the right support, you may be hard-pressed to overcome the overwhelming objections, overtly and covertly spoken, from those who are closest to you. Stand firm in your faith. Trust your gut. You have what it takes, and you do not require anyone's permission to pursue your healing.

Guilt will try to disgrace you

We find it hard to spend money on our desires when there are important bills to be paid. We can't possibly be out gathering wildflowers when there are dishes to be done. We work hard to create and perpetuate our happy homes and gardens and relationships, and that means sacrifice and being an adult.

As women, our need for esteeming others affects our whole being. We gain our self-worth from valuing and serving others over ourselves. We want others to get what they want out of life, so we are supportive, giving, and cooperative. It would be devastating to many of us to be thought of as selfish, greedy, or indulgent.

As a result, we often diminish and dismiss our own desires. We find it hard to say no when someone needs our help. We find it hard to vote for sushi when someone else wants Italian. We'll go see *Star Wars* instead of *Beauty and the Beast* if that's what they would rather do. We find it hard to put our own oxygen mask on before assisting the person next to us.

In the weeks leading up to my Walkabout, I was nearly crushed by this sense of guilt. How could I put my wedding on hold? How could I abandon my mom? How could I be disloyal to the family business? I was ashamed by my selfishness. Was I even a good person anymore? Was I ever a good person at all?

The truth of the matter was that I had given so much of myself that I was empty. I had nothing left to give. And I had begun resenting others for needing more from me. I was exhausted and angry, and I was hiding in plain sight. I was not present and available to the people I loved. I was just going through the motions and trying not to fall flat on my face.

It takes great courage and love and to recognize and honor your own needs and desires. A part of you knows this is important, but it feels impossible to put into action. You need to meet the little girl within and see the tears in her eyes. When does she get to be the most important thing in your life? When does she get to be loved and honored and cared for? Do you intend to keep her locked away forever?

Think of all the times your deep Self has gone without, taken the blame, stepped up to the plate, been a good girl, has done whatever it takes to make people happy and proud. It is not selfish to cherish her. It is kind and caring and beautiful. Remember this. Take a stand for your own Self and feel amazing about it.

Perfectionism will try to trap you

If you are anything like me, you probably take pride in your perfectionism. Our deepest personal worth is often tied to what we are able to achieve. The more perfect we can be, the better we feel about ourselves. The more perfect we can be, the better we are able to avoid pain, or so we tell ourselves. If pain comes anyway, it was because we (or someone else) weren't perfect enough.

If you can find a way to break free of fear, stigma, and guilt, perfectionism will be waiting as your final snare, and it is rarely unsuccessful in its trappings. It says things like:

- "It's not the right time. I need to wait for _____."
- "I have to get in shape first."

- "I'm too old."
- "The world is such a crazy place now."

Perfectionism will feed you exactly what you need to hear to keep you from moving forward TODAY. Believe me, there is no time like the present. In fact, there is literally no time BUT the present. If you want the future you dream of, you get it by taking action. And NOW is the only moment in which you can act. Don't fall for the promise of tomorrow being any better than your present opportunity. Accept that things are going to be messy, you are going to be messy, and that is okay. In fact, it's perfect.

Conclusion

"A dangerous woman delves deeply into the truth of who she is, grounds herself daily in the healing and empowering love of God, and radically engages with the needs of the world."

—LYNNE HYBELS

I had constructed a life that was safe and responsible. The imperfect, impetuous daughter had grown into the model female, putting everyone's needs before her own. And I was proud of myself for doing it. The accolades I earned further reinforced my belief system that what mattered most in life was getting everything right and serving everyone with grace. My worth was tied to this belief system. The more perfect and people-pleasing I could be, the better I felt about myself and my life. It was a debilitating way to live, but it was the only life that was modeled for me, the only life I knew.

I am grateful for the divine disorder that finally set me on my journey. I could never have imagined the things I would learn about myself and about our world and about our power as women along the way. What I have come to believe is that my inexplicable urge for travel and adventure was the call of the Wild meeting the yearning of my deep inner Self to be set free. On this journey to the truth of who I am, I discovered what I think of as the three levels of courage.

The three levels of courage

The first level of courage is Primal. Primal courage is all about survival. The fight or flight response is an example of primal courage. We don't have to think about it. Our brains and our bodies leap into action. When we are in survival mode, we quickly adapt skills and mindsets that will keep us safe. These skills and mindsets serve us for a time, but we often cling to them long after their usefulness has passed. I realized that I had spent most of my life in survival mode, exercising primal courage.

Fortunately, we can access the second level of courage and become Brave. When we are brave, we are taking some calculated risks. Part of the lure of adventure is that the outcome is uncertain. I entered this level of courage when I got in my car and drove into the unknown. Bravery is like a muscle that increases in strength as it is used appropriately. I was doing things that felt dangerous, but every time I successfully handled a risk, I grew in bravery. I began to trust my instincts as much as I trusted my intellect. I learned that I could navigate the unpredictable and that I did not have to be a slave to fear.

I learned things about my Self that surprised and delighted me. There was no one to serve but my Self, so I started asking Sonya what *she* needed. There was no one else to please, so I started asking Sonya what pleased *her*. There was no one to direct my steps, so I decided for *myself* what *I* desired. I learned the truth of who I am, and I discovered that I *like* who I am. I learned what *I* need to function at my best, and I experienced the rush of peak performance, health and happiness.

I emerged a deeper person from this journey. I can balance making choices that serve others with those that serve my Self without feeling guilty. I am no longer desperately driven by the expectations of others to the detriment of my own wants and needs. I value my desires and give them a proper place in my life. I have become empowered, experiencing the third level of courage.

And guess what? I learned that being empowered, loving and serving my Self, was the most loving thing I could do for others. It may be too harsh to say that I regret the years I wavered in my refusal to answer the call of the Wild. I know every step I have taken was good and right in its own time. *But what if? What if I knew then what I know now?*

I believe the Wild calls to us women in a very special way. Within nature flows a healing salve for our deepest wounds. She offers keys that unlock the sacred doors to the hidden power within us. She wants to reveal the secrets of this power to the genuine seeker. She beckons us to come away, rest at her hem, and once again become the keepers of ancient truth and wisdom that flows from her, and through her, and through us. We are being called for such a time as this, when our world broods and aches for the rise of the feminine. We can find the courage to answer that call and be empowered by it.

This book is the voice of the Wild, whispering with symbol and tales, crafting her secret invitation to you. Each verse was delivered while I explored the outdoors in wild, natural spaces, written long by my own hand, moving the relic of pen over the parchment of paper. Every story I relate to you here was forged in a primal place where uncertainty met courage and deep resolve. My hope is that you feel this energy pulsing through these pages and recognize the same is pulsing through your own veins, coursing through your own brave heart.

Your dream come true

My wish is for you to find the truth of who you are, and that that truth will set you free. My wish is that you find that freedom sooner rather than later. I do not want you to spend one more year in suffering silence. GO. Dive deep with your Self. Have the epic adventure you have been dreaming of. Be daring and bold. Find your peace.

GO. Be free to love and cherish your Self. And after that, be free to radically engage with the needs of others. Be brave enough to listen to your heart and trust your instincts, knowing this is your ultimate service to the people you love. Author Sarah Ban Breathnach said it best, "The world needs dreamers and the world needs doers. But above all, the world needs dreamers who do."

You have permission to GO. Know that countless people are counting on you to be Wisely Wild, to show them what is possible, to give them a taste of freedom.

P.S. I love you

My greatest joy is hearing women share their stories. In doing so, we send down roots into the depths of our experience, and our life branches out to touch the world around us. It would be an honor to hear from you. Ask me questions, give me feedback, share your peaks and valleys. My email address is Sequoia1011@gmail.com.

GO Deeper

If you'd like to GO Deeper with me, I am now publishing my personal journal pages as companion reading—real, raw, and unedited. I will let you in on exactly what I was thinking and how I was feeling as each chapter of my sacred solo adventure unfolded. Do I have enough courage to "let the outside in and let my insides out" in total vulnerability? Visit GOSoloTravel.Life to find out, as I must decide, day by day, to publish what I printed in private.

I am also working on my second book, which chronicles what happened next, when my ten-week Walkabout turned into a sacred solo quest which lasted two full years. Details at GOSoloTravel.Life.

Afterword

Should I stay or should I go?

I always wanted to be the kind of person who stays. I wanted to be the kind of person who sticks it out when things get tough. I wanted to be the kind of person who sees the deep inner good and the highest potential, the kind of person who chooses to hold onto that good and love in spite of what may actually be happening at the surface.

I have always cheered for the underdog. I have loved the unlovable. I have endeavored to be the heart of God in this world, bringing love and light to dark places and to people who believe they are undeserving. I think I thought that made me noble in some way.

When I sacrifice myself for the good of another, doesn't that make me a good person? When I choose a life of poverty in order to serve the poor, to be counted among them, doesn't that prove how deeply I love them? When I choose to stay in a marriage that is violent and emotionally desolate, when I choose to give love in the face of fear and loathing, doesn't that prove how devoted I am? Doesn't everyone deserve to know they are loved, even at their worst? And when I am shrinking and dying inside, but I show up every day and do the work and put my best face forward and achieve the impossible, doesn't that show just how deep my love and loyalty goes?

I thought so. I thought giving and sacrificing myself proved my love. "For God so loved the world...." And so I gave and I gave and I gave. But an astonishing thing happened. The people I served stayed sick anyway. My love never lifted them up. My love actually gave them a reason to stay miserable. The homeless stayed homeless. The angry stayed angry. The broken stayed broken. The mean stayed mean.

There must be a better way.

Many years ago I received counsel from John Glenn, pastor of the Church in the Woods. I didn't understand it at the time. He told us, "You can't help everyone. You can only help those who are worthy."

"Who are the worthy?" we asked him.

"Those who WILL," he said.

Why is it we must come to the end of ourselves in order to begin anew? I thought my Walkabout had brought me to the edge of myself and beyond. Turns out, I keep finding new edges.

These three remain

My relationship with Edward eventually ended. It was difficult to let go of the story I wanted for us. I had dreams of happily ever after that always included him. Was it the distance that ended it for us? Or was it the distance that gave us enough clarity to see that we were very different people moving in very different directions?

I am so grateful for my time with Edward. If indeed adversity is meant to initiate us into greatness, then we have nothing to regret. Our journey has not ended; it has only begun. *The light in me honors the light in you.*

I am learning that *proving* my love, loyalty, and devotion through sacrifice is not necessary. Nor effective. It is enough to love. Love is powerful enough. It needs no proving to make it more so.

I could tell you that I have been deeply and radically changed, and this would be true. The paradox is that the change has been merely the interruption of illusion, so that the truth of who I am is what persists.

> *"These three remain: faith, hope and love. And the greatest of these is love."*
>
> 1 CORINTHIANS 13:13

Acknowledgments

To my constant companion, Justice. She is a Jack-Chi—totally springy like a Jack Russell and totally clingy like a Chihuahua. She is my trusty sidekick, my sleeping bag snuggler, my alert to any danger, my always *welcome back!*, and my hiking buddy with springs in her legs and a smile on her face. She is smart and mischievous and loves adventure as much as I do. This journey would not have been the same without you, baby girl. ♡

To my son, Cameron and my grandson, Grayson—the only two *boys* with the power to save me from myself. I was walking a dangerous road when I became pregnant, and I blessed the day I discovered I had something remarkable to live for—his name would be Cameron. Being your mom is a grand adventure! I was treading on dangerous ground once again when another baby boy performed his marvelous intervention. His name would be Grayson. Destination Grayson became my Walkabout, an incredible journey of hope, healing, and transformation. This book is that journey.

To the man who has punctuated my story in so many ways. Thank you for believing that I had a book in me and doing everything in your power to get it out of me, short of gluing the pen in my hand and locking me in the garret. You have been a strong tower of support for this book and this author-in-transformation. Cheers to the tale of us, Edward.

To Dr. Angela Lauria of The Author Incubator, for helping me accomplish in nine weeks what I could not do on my own in nine months. I am indebted to you for helping me go beyond just writing a bunch of words on paper, but to author a book that can actually make a difference. I am further grateful that you helped me dig deep inside and discover that my words held a message that could change lives. You inspired the courage I needed to come out of hiding—to let the outside in and my insides out. Any woman who benefits from my service will be linked to yours.

To the awesome ladies at Adventure Some Women, especially Natalie McCarthy of Ask Natalie. Thank you for the hours you spent with me during the research phase of this book project. Thank you for letting me bounce ideas around the group and offering meaningful feedback. I appreciate your candor, guts, and authenticity. I look forward to seeing you all getting your brave on with your posts and pics. I can hardly wait for our next adventure! AdventureSomeWomen.com and facebook.com/groups/adventuresomewomen

And to the dear friends who offered me respite on my travels. I am deeply grateful for your hospitality and companionship. Thank you for sharing the little things that make such a big difference—fresh towels, home-cooked meals, goodnight hugs. You opened your homes and your hearts to me, and I want you to know what an important role you played in my journey. I visited each you by divine appointment, and you each had an invaluable message that I needed to receive. While this book is about my solo road trip, I know that I was never really alone, and I remember fondly our short time together.

Pop—Walla Walla, WA
Brenna—Portland, OR
Mark & Alison—West Hills, CA
Uncle David—Phoenix, AZ
Tanya—Santa Fe, NM
Angie—Carnegie, OK
Teresa—Oklahoma City
John—Wellsville, KS
Kathee—Mason City, IA
My BFF Cathy—Madison, VA
James & Pamela—RVA
Dad & Nancy—Myrtle Beach, SC
Melinda—Columbus, GA
Cameron & Julia—Vero Beach, FL
Jim & Karen—Vero Beach, FL

I have always lived my life with the sense that my story is being written with every choice I make. I believed I could make a difference for those who were watching me, reading my story as I walked it out. This final acknowledgement is for you, dear Reader, my Facebook friend, Instagram follower, or blog commenter. You are the person who inspires me to do the hard stuff, to speak my truth, and to live each day with courage. I believe in you.

About the Author

"Send danger from the east unto the west,
So honor cross it from the north to south,
And let them grapple."

—William Shakespeare

SONYA LOUISE

Life can be hard, and starting life at the poverty line, even harder. Labeled strong-willed and rebellious, Sonya addressed her first growing pangs of divine disorder by leaving home at age 15 with only her dreams and determination in hand.

Her first jobs were in fast food, and she quickly ascended to management. A natural overachiever, what she lacked in education she surpassed with ingenuity and, relying on grace and grit, she moved from industry to industry, conquering the nuances of each, looking for greater

147

advancement and ways to make a meaningful contribution to the world.

At age 30, she moved to Florida and volunteered at the local homeless shelter. Eight years later she became executive director and championed the community's first housing program for single adults.

At age 40, she moved to the Pacific Northwest and began working at a family winery, launching a new tasting room (complete with gourmet cheese counter) and eventually becoming director of hospitality and sales. Sonya was poised to become majority owner, but she felt deeply unfulfilled. She could tell herself that her work was making people happy, but she knew that pouring wine was not really making a difference.

Sonya had long been intrigued by the idea of personal pilgrimage and by stories of those who had been transformed by this kind of journey. In August 2016, at 43 years old, she embarked on a solo road trip that led her over 10,000 miles in 10 weeks, into wild places, to the edge of herself and beyond. Stripped of non-essentials and distractions, Sonya discovered what was truly important and recovered her life's calling.

An entrepreneur with a deep sense of social justice, Sonya's journey provides a road map for all women learning to tap into a more adventurous way of living. Her challenge to all of us is to discover our own wild sense of joy and wonder.

Email: Sequoia1011@gmail.com
Facebook: facebook.com/sequoia101
Instagram: @sequoia1011

Thank You

Your Gift: A free medicine card reading

Something drew you to this book. Something made you keep reading; following me on this epic adventure. You made a choice with your time and invested your energy here. Could it be that you are ready to embark on a sacred solo journey of your own? Do you feel the Call of your own inner Wild? Why do you think that is?

A medicine card reading can help you find the answers. Native peoples understood our deep connection to Nature and believed the animals to be our teachers and messengers. I have been using medicine cards to help deepen my own knowledge of how Nature and the animals communicate with us—and how these messages can offer clarity and wisdom when we are standing at the crossroads.

A medicine card reading can reveal to you information about the overall pathway of your life. Through this reading, you are able to:

- see your present pathway
- see where you have been

- see where you are going
- see what is challenging you
- see what you have completed

I am offering a free medicine card reading as my way of saying Thank You for sharing this piece of your life with me. To claim your free pathway reading, simply email me at Sequoia1011@gmail.com with the subject line: Medicine Card Reading.